ESSAYS ON PHOTOGRAPHY

THE UNKNOWN CONAN DOYLE

—◆—

ESSAYS ON PHOTOGRAPHY

—◆—

COMPILED WITH AN INTRODUCTION BY
JOHN MICHAEL GIBSON AND
RICHARD LANCELYN GREEN

Secker & Warburg
Distributed by David & Charles, Inc.
North Pomfret, Vermont 05053

This edition first published in England 1982 by
Martin Secker & Warburg Limited
54 Poland Street, London W1V 3DF

Introduction and notes © 1982 by John Michael Gibson
and Richard Lancelyn Green

British Library Cataloguing in Publication Data
Doyle, *Sir* Arthur Conan
Essays on photography.
1. Photograph – Addresses, essays, lectures
I. Title   II. Gibson, J.M.   III. Green, Richard
Lancelyn
770   TR185

ISBN 0-436-13302-4

Typeset by Inforum Ltd, Portsmouth
Printed and bound in Great Britain by
The Pitman Press, Bath

CONTENTS

———◆———

FOREWORD

One of the richest rewards of bibliography is that the research reveals so much that has passed into oblivion. When we embarked on the enormous task of listing and describing Conan Doyle's collected and uncollected writings, we did not expect to find either the quality or quantity of unknown and forgotten work that we did. Our most exciting discovery was these early contributions to the *British Journal of Photography*.

For this volume we have selected all the pieces on photography which Conan Doyle wrote as a young man. The first was published before he left Edinburgh in 1881, and the last shortly after his marriage in 1885. We have also included the description of the voyage to West Africa written in 1923, as this assumes a new complection when seen in the context of his three early articles on the same subject.

John Michael Gibson
Richard Lancelyn Green

INTRODUCTION

The obituary articles which appeared after Arthur Conan Doyle's death in July 1930 concentrated for the most part on his books. He was the author of the historical novels, *Micah Clarke* and *The White Company*, of *Rodney Stone* which had done much to popularise boxing, and the creator of memorable characters like Brigadier Gerard, Professor Challenger, and, above all, Sherlock Holmes. He was also remembered for his attempts to secure justice for George Edalji and Oscar Slater, his histories of the Boer War and the Great War, his propaganda booklet, *The War in South Africa*, which had led to a knighthood, his efforts on behalf of the Congo natives, and for many similar activities. There was also the belief in spiritualism which had dominated his thoughts since 1916 and taken him all over the country and abroad to Australia, America, Africa, and Scandinavia explaining the "new revelation", and had led him to establish a Psychic Bookshop and Museum and finance the Psychic Press.

The columns of the obituary notices were too short to list all his works, but there was little need to do so as the majority were still in print and his autobiography, *Memories and Adventures*, had recently been reissued by John Murray. It was there that many looked for details of his early years, and no one noticed that there were gaps when it came to his childhood in Edinburgh or his days in Southsea as a doctor. A few of the obituaries did contain original material from people who had known Doyle in unusual circumstances or who recalled an aspect of his life that was not generally known. This was the case with the "Ex Cathedra" note in the *British Journal of Photography* on 11 July 1930, for it mentioned that he had been an early contributor whose first article had appeared in 1881, though the significance of the articles was not recognised. They had been in oblivion for nearly fifty years and were to be so again.

Doyle never mentioned the articles after he had left Southsea. It was not that he had forgotten about them – he had the proofs of one and a copy of another pasted into his first scrapbook which he used when he wrote his autobiography – but rather that he wished to suppress some details of the hardship and poverty of his early years: the fact that his family had been forced to rely on the charity of a local lady and that his father was an alcoholic who had spent the last years of his life in various mental institutions. He therefore passed over the connection between his and the Burton family, and this included his own friendship with W.K. Burton who had first introduced him to photography and may have suggested that he write the articles. He might also have felt that as one of the early contributions made unflattering references to psychic phenomena, it would be inadvisable to draw attention to it.

Arthur Conan Doyle was born on 22 May 1859 in a small rented flat at 11 Picardy Place. His father, Charles Altamont Doyle, the son of John Doyle (known as "H.B.") and brother of Richard Doyle, had moved to Edinburgh in 1849 to take up a position as second clerk in H.M. Office of Works. He lodged with an Irish Catholic lady, Mrs. Foley, and in 1855 married her daughter Mary. She bore him ten children of whom seven survived. The size of the family would have stretched the resources of a man better paid than Charles Doyle. Although he earned a little extra from his drawings, his salary was low. Money was short and survival difficult, even, at times, sordid.

Soon after Arthur was born, the family moved to Tower Bank House, Portobello, and later to 3 Sciennes Hill Place, but the happiest part of the boy's childhood was spent at Liberton Bank, a cottage owned by Mary Burton. It was from here that he attended his first school, the Newington Academy.

Mary Burton, the sister of John Hill Burton,[1] had moved to Liberton Bank with her mother in 1844, after her brother's marriage. Her mother died a few years later, but she continued to live there, without marrying, until the 1880s. She was a lady of a charitable disposition and was always surrounded by friends and relations. Her brother, John, worked for the prison service but was also a well-known literary figure and a great book collector. He was the author of an exhaustive *History of Scotland* and of *The Book Hunter* for which he is now best remembered. In 1855, six years after the death of his first wife, he married Katherine Innes, the daughter of the Scottish antiquary Cosmo Innes. They had four children of whom the eldest son, William Kinnimond

Burton was to become one of Conan Doyle's earliest and closest friends. The boys probably first met at Liberton Bank and, though often separated, kept in close touch at least until 1887.

William Burton was born in May 1856. He attended the Edinburgh Collegiate School and in 1873 was apprenticed for five years to Brown Brothers and Company, hydraulic and mechanical engineers at the Rosebank Ironworks, where he became the chief draughtsman in 1878.

The introduction of the dry plate or gelatine-bromide process a few years earlier heralded a new epoch in photography and led to a revival of interest. William and his brother, Cosmo Innes Burton, who was eight years younger, both took up the subject with enthusiasm, derived perhaps from their grandfather, Professor Cosmo Innes, who had been one of the earliest photographers, working with the paper processes of the 1860s; their enthusiasm was also shared by A.B. Brown of Brown Brothers. Most of the boys' childhood had been spent at Craighouse, but in 1879 the family moved to Morton House and they were allowed the use of a tower called the Belvidere which they converted into a workshop and laboratory. Conan Doyle probably visited them there and that may have been his earliest introduction to photography.

William Burton applied for membership of the Edinburgh Photographic Society at the end of 1879 and was elected on 7 January 1880. His brother followed on 4 February, A.B. Brown on 3 March, and another friend, A.P. Lawrie, on 7 April. Thereafter they attended many meetings of the society and continued to make experiments on their own. By December, when Cosmo and Lawrie presented their first paper, William had moved to London. He left Brown Brothers to go into partnership with his uncle, Cosmo Innes, a civil engineer who had worked on the railways in Britain and India before being disabled in an accident. The decision followed the Public Health Conference of June 1880 which had drawn attention to the inadequate sanitary arrangements in old houses and the need for higher standards in new ones. William was the junior partner in the firm of Innes and Burton, Consulting Engineers, which had an office in the Adelphi at 7 John Street where certificates for new buildings could be procured and tests on old ones arranged.[2]

During this period Conan Doyle was at the Jesuit College of Stonyhurst; he spent two years in the junior school of Hodder and then five years in the main college. After a further year at Feldkirch in Austria, he enrolled in 1876 as a student at Edinburgh University to read medicine. He lived with his parents in

George Square and spent part of his vacations gaining experience with doctors in Sheffield and Shropshire, and later working as a paid assistant to Dr. Reginald Ratcliffe Hoare in Birmingham. He took eight months leave during 1880 to go as a surgeon on an Arctic whaler. After he became a Bachelor of Medicine and Master of Surgery in the summer of 1881, he had to consider his future. The idea of serving as a naval surgeon appealed to him, but he decided to continue his practical training with Dr. Hoare until a suitable opening arose.

It was while he was with Dr. Hoare in 1879 that he had his first short story accepted by *Chambers's Journal*, and the following year he placed another with *London Society*, a magazine in which his father had had work published. He had also by then written a great deal of poetry and was prepared to turn his hand to any subject, whether national politics, medical discoveries, translations from the German, or general articles.

Burton returned to Edinburgh in summer of 1881 to be at his father's bedside during his final illness. He probably saw Doyle and told him about his photographic work in London. He was already a regular contributor to the *Photographic News* and the *British Journal of Photography*. The latter, in which all Doyle's articles were to appear, had started life as the *Liverpool Photographic Journal* on 15 January 1854, four years before the *Photographic News*. After being known by various names, it became the *British Journal of Photography* in January 1860 and has continued as such to this day, being the oldest surviving photographic journal in the world. It was originally a monthly, then a fortnightly, and from 1865 a weekly. W.B. Bolton was the editor during the period that Doyle was a contributor having taken over from John Traill Taylor who went to America at the end of 1878. Bolton held the position until Taylor's return in 1885 when he became an associate editor. He was a close friend of Burton and they did many experiments together in the magazine's offices in York Street, only a few minutes walk from Burton's lodgings. This would have enabled Burton to recommend Doyle's work or at least to know that it would be sympathetically considered.

The new editor began a series of articles in 1880 under the general heading "Where to Go with the Camera". These were descriptions of places of scenic beauty giving details of views, or "bits" as they were then known, which would make good photographic subjects. It proved so popular with the readers that the editor decided to continue the series in June 1881. He noted in his column that the previous articles had been unsolicited and expressed the hope that "we may be able to secure as much assistance from volunteers as we did last year, in order to enable us to keep up the weekly succession of articles." This may have inspired Doyle's first contribution, a description of a visit to the Isle of May. It showed that he already had a firm grasp of the principles of photography and of the contents of recent numbers of the journal. It also provides a fascinating insight into his reading at this time. The style and format appear to be derived from Mark Twain, whose works are referred to on a number of occasions. The influence of Oliver Wendell Holmes is also evident, the use of *sobriquets* like "The Man of Science" and much of the humour is clearly based on the Breakfast-Table series. All the articles contain allusions, whether to the classics, or the work of contemporary English and American writers, or popular songs, or the work of local artists.

Doyle's first article, "After Cormorants with a Camera", appeared in two halves on 14 and 21 October 1881, and this coincided with his departure for the West Coast of Africa. It was more successful than anyone could have envisaged as it caught the attention of the editor of *Anthony's Photographic Bulletin* in New York, who reprinted the piece commenting that the British photographic journals had "well-written and entertaining descriptions of what, in their peculiar way, they call *outings*, and we do not see why some of our serious amateurs do not occasionally treat themselves to an outing". This was the earliest piece by Doyle to be published in America and is perhaps appropriate as it includes a reference to a friend called Holmes, his first known use of a name which he was to make famous on both sides of the Atlantic. The praise which the Americans bestowed certainly impressed the editor who was happy to take Doyle's subsequent articles about his experiences in West Africa, and later in Devon, Southsea, Ireland, and Arran. As well as a letter, Doyle also contributed two technical articles, the first of which, written in October 1882, appeared in the *British Journal Photographic Almanac* for 1883. Doyle was again approached the following year but by then was too busy. He told his Edinburgh friend, Mrs. Drummond: "I am up to my eyes in work. There are my own people to be looked after. Then a neighbouring medico has gone away for a month and I take the Parish for him. Then there is the lecture to be written and many maps to be drawn. The Photographic Journal are simply howling for an article for their almanac – and I am going in for the Seven roomed house which is offered by Tit Bits for the best Xmas story." His lecture to the Portsmouth Literary and Scientific Society proved a notable success, but he failed in his bid to win the house and did not submit an article for the 1884 almanac.

William Burton soon made a name for himself in photographic circles. He was elected to the Photographic Society on 8 November 1881, joined most of the other important photographic societies, and was himself later instrumental in the founding of the Camera Club. Articles by him appeared in most of the journals; those in the *Photographic News* on the basic processes were reprinted in 1882 as *The ABC of Modern Photography* which became one of the most popular handbooks of the day.

The intimacy which existed between the Doyle and Burton families is shown by the name which Mary Doyle chose for one of her daughters who was christened Caroline Mary Burton Doyle.[3] That between Arthur Conan Doyle and William Burton is apparent in the articles themselves. In "After Cormorants with a Camera", Doyle refers to a " 'dodge' communicated to me by my friend, Mr. W.K. Burton". This was the use of a cabinet mount cut with an aperture to produce good cloud effects in imperfect light. Burton is mentioned in "A Few Technical Hints", while the piece which followed was a description of the emulsion process which Burton had described at a meeting of the Photographic Society. Doyle promised an unprejudiced trial as the process was still *sub judice* "though introduced by my friend Mr. W.K. Burton as far back as the 14th November . . .". Burton was also indebted to Doyle. In "Precipitation Methods and Green Fog", which appeared in the *British Journal of Photography* on 26 January 1883, he remarks: "Another defect likely to arise from too great alkalinity of an emulsion is the superficial chemical fog which I described some time ago. I have to thank Dr. A. Conan Doyle for pointing out that this fog is really caused by alkalinity of an emulsion which has a predisposition to the defect. I now always neutralise – or rather render again acid – the emulsion with which I am just about to coat the plates."

Doyle does not appear to have belonged to any photographic society, nor to have known many of the leading photographers of the day. There is, though, a proposed visit which is mentioned in a letter to Mrs. Drummond which is also of interest as it throws some light on his self-designed tripod. That, it seems, existed more tangibly on paper than it did elsewhere. The undated letter, probably written in 1883, runs: "Willie Burton writes me a pleasing item. He was at supper yesterday with Henry Greenwood proprietor of the Photographic News and several other photographic swells. The conversation turned upon me and he very imprudently launched out into some reminiscences of our sayings and doings together which tickled the company so much that H.G. then and there announced his intention of coming down to Southsea expressly to see me, and the company in a body volunteered to go with him. So I have the pleasant prospect of a roomful of photographers clamouring to see my negatives and my wonderful Unipod stand – which has been described so often tho' mortal eye has never seen it." Whether the visit took place is not known.

The letter will help to show how Doyle composed his articles. He was obviously free to enhance them with reports of spectacular photographs and success in difficult shots. He also appears to have re-shaped his own experiences to suit the occasion. He had a quick eye for detail and was already adept at using maps and timetables to give authenticity. Where his journey, for example, had begun from his house in Southsea, in the article he would bring the reader down from London on a particular train, lodge him in a good hotel, and after the visit return him to the fog-bound metropolis. The friends were also chosen as types, though many would have recognised themselves and a number of real people appear under their own names. Whether Doyle in fact took a camera to all the places he describes is not known, though it seems unlikely.

No photographs by Doyle are known to exist from this period, though there is one which shows Bush Villa, his house in Southsea, which may be by him (or possibly of him). Either the photographs did not exist, in which case he demonstrated an extremely fertile imagination, or they did exist as stated but were subsequently either lost or destroyed by chemical decomposition. In the July 1882 number of *Good Words*, A.A. Campbell-Swinton in an article on "Recent Advances in Photography" perhaps supplies the answer: "Most, if not all people have bitter remembrances of what were once beautiful photographs, but which now, alas! are but sickly, yellow, and faded phantoms of their former selves. The instability of ordinary silver prints on albumenised paper is well known, and is a defect unhappily inherent in the process, at least experience seems to prove it so." This could explain the loss of Doyle's photographs. The early developers and hand-coated emulsions were unstable, but many photographs did survive. There is one in Doyle's first scrapbook which he began in August 1885. It is contemporary and shows a flash of lightning taken by Dr. Puddicombe, R.N. It is in fine condition and demonstrates the excellence of the gelatine plate and the "instantaneous" shutter. It has survived as have many by other people, so perhaps Doyle's photographs will one day come to light.

Doyle's photographic articles stopped in 1885. There were various reasons for this. His marriage on 6 August had changed his Bohemian existence into one of settled calm and domestic order, the editorship of the *British Journal of Photography* had reverted to John Traill Taylor whose policy was different to that of W.B. Bolton, and Doyle was spending more time on fiction. Early in 1884 he had begun a sensational novel called "Girdlestone and Co." which he wrote while waiting for his patients. He had done half by the time of his marriage and completed it in November 1885. No publisher was prepared to take it; four years were to elapse before it was accepted by a newspaper syndicate on the strength of *A Study in Scarlet* and *Micah Clarke* and only on condition that parts were revised. After this had been done in September 1889, the novel began a weekly serialisation in the *People* and was published by Chatto and Windus in April 1890 as *The Firm of Girdlestone*. The novel is of interest here because of the dedication. The author had been encouraged to write the book by William Burton and it was to him that he dedicated it: "To My Old Friend / Professor William K. Burton, / of the Imperial University, Tokio, / who first encouraged me, years ago, to proceed with / this little story, / I desire affectionately to / dedicate it. / The Author."

Burton had left England in 1887 having been appointed Professor of Sanitary Engineering and Lecturer on Rivers, Docks and Harbours in the College of Engineering at the Imperial University in Tokyo. He was given a farewell banquet by the *British Journal of Photography* at Holborn Restaurant on 30 March 1887, which nearly all his friends attended. In 1888, as well as his professorship, he became a consulting engineer on Water and Sewerage Works to the Japanese Home Department and was to design works for many Japanese and Formosan towns. He became fluent in Japanese soon after his arrival, and his interest in photography enabled him to play an important part in its development in Japan. He was closely associated with the Photographic Society of Japan and established the dry plate factory of Burton and Kajima. His assistants, like K. Arito, became proficient photographers whose work was much admired in Europe. Burton also continued to contribute to the British photographic journals, writing descriptions of his travels in Japan. He collaborated with John Milne, a close friend who was the Professor of Seismology at the Imperial University, on a book about the great earthquake of 1891. He also wrote a number of technical books on photography, supplied photographs for books on Japanese life, and was the author of a standard textbook on *The Water*

Supply of Towns. He died in Tokyo at the beginning of August 1899 from a malarial complaint.[4] Although not yet fifty, he had outlived his younger brother who had died in the Far East a few years earlier. The obituary notice for W.K. Burton in the *British Journal of Photography* described him as "a perfect type of the painstaking and experimental photographer, with a happy gift of being able to transmit his knowledge to others". A sentiment with which Doyle would, no doubt, have concurred. Although Burton's exposure tables and his handbook on photography were still in use, his contribution to the development of photography had been limited and was already superseded by later improvements.

Doyle's later experiences with photography are separate from his early work. Like thousands of others, he became an enthusiastic amateur photographer during the next decade. He had left Southsea in 1890 to visit Berlin in order to write a report for W.T. Stead's *Review of Reviews* on Dr. Koch's tuberculosis cure. On the journey out he met Malcolm Morris who persuaded him to specialise. He therefore went to Vienna at the end of the year to study the eye with the intention of setting up in London as an eye consultant. He had always been interested in the subject and had spent much of his free time doing voluntary work with Dr. A. Vernon Ford at the Portsmouth and South Hants Eye and Ear Infirmary. The interest in optics was obviously useful in photography (as it was years later in the Edalji case) but this does not appear to have entered Doyle's mind at the time.

After his return to England, he opened a consulting room at 2 Upper Wimpole Street, but clients were few and far between so he wrote to fill the time. The first six adventures of Sherlock Holmes, which he started in April 1891, proved so popular that he was soon able to give up his eye practice. When he wrote to his mother on 14 October 1891 from his new address at 12 Tennison Road, South Norwood, to say that the *Strand Magazine* had implored him to continue the series and that he would do so if they offered him £50 for each, irrespective of length, he also told her: "I sold my eye instruments for £6.10.0 with which I shall buy photographic apparatus, so we have been able to start a hobby without any outlay." Although five years had elapsed, and his old equipment, if he still had it, would have been out of date, it is still odd that he should talk of "starting" a hobby. Whatever the explanation, he entered on it with enthusiasm. When Harry How called on him in June 1892, he noted that Doyle was a "capital amateur photographer", and the evidence of this ability survives – though the two photograph albums among the archives do not, perhaps, represent his finest work. They cover the period from 1890 to 1898 and include snap-shots of his two children in the garden at 12 Tennison Road and of friends like Jerome K. Jerome. The first album also contains photographs of his skiing holiday in Switzerland,[5] some of which were used to illustrate an article in *Pearson's Magazine* in 1897. Although the photographs were redrawn, the article is itself of some interest as it was by D.G. Thomson, a friend whom Doyle met at the Royal Edinburgh Infirmary, who was also an early contributor to the *British Journal of Photography*. The later album includes photographs of Doyle's new house at Hindhead while it was being built. The albums are, as the titles on them imply, a very miscellaneous collection. Many of the photographs are by other people, but a few of these do show Doyle holding a camera.

Although there are occasional references to photography in Doyle's work, it does not have any prominence. There is an interesting reference in the early story, "The Recollections of Captain Wilkie" in which the narrator applies the methods of an Edinburgh Professor in an attempt to analyse the character of the man seated opposite him in a railway compartment: "No red acid spots upon his clothes, no ink-stains, no nitrate-of-silver marks upon his hands (this helps to negative my half-formed opinion that he was a photographer) . . ." Sherlock Holmes never used a camera, despite the development of the miniature "detective" cameras concealed in binoculars, watches, and hats which were popular at the time. The first reference in the Sherlock Holmes stories comes in "The Red-Headed League" when Jabez Wilson informs Holmes that his assistant, Vincent Spaulding, has his faults: "Never was there such a fellow for photography. Snapping away with his camera when he ought to be improving his mind, and then diving down into the cellar like a rabbit into its bolt hole to develop his pictures." But this was to deceive the pawnbroker about the real reason he was spending so much time in the cellar. If photography itself did not serve as an influence, Doyle's friendship with Burton may, at least, have provided the details for "The Adventure of the Engineer's Thumb", and may explain Doyle's ambition to be a civil engineer, which provoked his master to reply: "You may be an engineer, Doyle, but from what I have seen of you I should think it very unlikely that you will be a civil one."

Between the turn of the century and the Great War, the only photographs Doyle took were snap-shots of his second family. The large albums which lined his shelves contained the work of other photographers. There were pictures of the field hospital in

South Africa, where he had been a volunteer physician, presented by Langman, of his stage plays like *The Fires of Fate*, and various studio portraits. The one notable incursion into photography was his faked illustrations for *The Lost World*. Not only did he portray Professor Challenger under a heavy beard and expert make-up by Willy Clarkson, but he also, with the assistance of W. Ransford, made the photographs of the plateau by pasting two photographs together.

After the War his interest in photography reasserted itself though his concern was then with the possibilities and validity of psychic photography. During the remaining years of his life he built up one of the largest collections of psychic photographs in the world, which he used in a number of lectures and displayed prominently in the museum attached to the Psychic Bookshop which he established in 1925.

The first authentic psychic or "spirit" photograph was generally believed to have been taken in Boston by William H. Mumler in 1861. The earliest verified example in England was taken in 1872 by John Beattie of Bristol who achieved "extras" in that year; his honesty was vouched for by John Traill Taylor, the editor of the *British Journal of Photography*. Taylor himself secured supernormal results a year later with Dr. Alfred Russell Wallace. Doyle had personal experience of two mediums capable of taking spirit photographs. These were Mrs. Deane, who was best known for her Armistice Day photographs (the first taken in 1922), and William Hope of the Crewe Circle. It was in Hope's defence that Doyle and Fred Barlow, the secretary of the Society for the Study of Supernormal Pictures, prepared the booklet *The Case for Spirit Photography* in 1922. Doyle had first visited Hope in Crewe during the summer of 1919, and on that occasion, to prevent the possibility of fraud after the photographs had been taken, he took out the plates with his own hands, developed them and fixed them. He also tested Mrs. Deane in February 1926. Her photographs were the subject of some ridicule in the popular press as the "extras" were judged to be members of a living football team. Doyle added a footnote to *The History of Spiritualism* stating that "the author has tested the medium with his own plates, marked and developed by himself. He obtained six psychic results in eight experiences." His own explanation of spirit photography was that some invisible intelligence built up the image within a containing envelope or "psychic cocoon".

One of the most famous psychic photographs with which Doyle dealt was the "Combermere Photograph". This had been taken in December 1891 on the afternoon of the funeral of the 2nd

Viscount Combermere and purported to show his legless "ghost" seated in a chair. After Doyle had mentioned it in a lecture at the Queen's Hall in 1926, he was drawn into a long controversy with A.A. Campbell Swinton, whose aunt had married the second Viscount Combermere, and whose interest in photography, like Doyle's own, dated back to the 1880s. Their correspondence ran through the columns of the *Morning Post*, the *Daily Sketch*, the *Sunday Times*, and *Nature*. At the end of it, Swinton still believed that it was a fraud, while Doyle was convinced that it was the "best case upon record of supernormal photography in ordinary life, without the use of the peculiar atmosphere of a developed pyschic photographer".

The most bizarre photographs with which Doyle was associated were the Cottingley fairy photographs. These were first sent to E.L. Gardner who then contacted Doyle; together they prepared an article for the 1920 *Strand Magazine* Christmas number, which later served as the basis for *The Coming of the Fairies*. The photographs had been taken in 1917 by two young girls whose truthfulness Doyle was not inclined to question. The belief in, or at least portrayal of, fairies was not new to the Doyle family. His father's drawings had frequently included fairies, as had those of his uncle, Richard Doyle, whose design for the cover of *Punch* was particularly well known. One of Conan Doyle's earliest poems, called "In Memoriam", which was written after his uncle's death in 1883, concerned the reaction of the fairies in Richard Doyle's drawings when his corpse was placed in his studio. Doyle had prepared an article on fairies before he knew of the existence of the Cottingley photographs. It was called "The Evidence for Fairies" and was to have appeared in the December 1920 issue of the *Strand Magazine*, though it was held over until March of the following year. Doyle remained interested in the subject for the rest of his life and reissued *The Coming of the Fairies* with additional photographs in 1928.

When Doyle was visited at his house in the New Forest by John Lewis, the editor of the *International Psychic Gazette*, at the beginning of September 1928, his first suggestion was that they might visit a local man who was a "friend of the fairies". The article which Lewis subsequently wrote for the *Cape Argus* (it also appeared in the *Gazette*) contains an extraordinary description of the garden at Bignell Wood with its "life" size pottery images of fairies and gnomes, for as he explained: "By cultivating the fairies Sir Arthur hopes some day to photograph them himself. The housekeeper at 'Bignell Wood' has a little eight-year-old daughter whom Sir Arthur sets occasionally on the stump of an old tree on the forest side of the garden gate with a musical box going full song, while he waits with a Kodak ready to snap one of these elusive sprites!"

Psychic photography has little relevance to photography either as an art or as a science. The best examples are shadowy and the "extras" are superimposed without logic and in defiance of the rules of science. Doyle, however, discounted conventional arguments whether they came from the *Scientific American* or from Kodak. The writer who had criticised W. Harding Warner's psychic force "Od" in 1883 and who had established himself in Wimpole Street as an eye specialist was able to speculate in *The Wanderings of a Spiritualist* that "the clairvoyant seems to be not a person with a better developed physical retina, but rather one who has the power to use that which corresponds with the retina in their own etheric bodies which are in harmony with etheric waves from outside". During a tour of America in 1923 he visited Rochester, which he said should be called "Eastman Town or Kodak Town, for that industry completely dominates it", but he showed no interest in visiting the Eastman House, preferring instead to pay his respects at the Fox House in Hydesville where spiritualism had been born in 1848.

William Burton in his photographic handbook suggested that a knowledge of science and an appreciation of art were the two requisites for the photographer. Doyle had possessed both, but at the end of his life each in turn was sacrificed on the altar of the supernormal. But whatever the fate of his later writings on psychic photography, the early writings on pure photography deserve to be better known. They are reprinted here for the first time since their original appearance, and, so far as is known, have only been mentioned once before this century in the brief obituary article in the *British Journal of Photography*. Doyle's major biographers, who must have seen copies in his scrapbook, failed to mention them or even to refer to his friendship with W.K. Burton, so it is hoped that this volume will shed some new light on Conan Doyle both as a man and as a writer, and that it will appeal alike to students of photography, local historians, and those with an interest in the author or in his famous creation, Sherlock Holmes. Whatever the defects, they are far outweighed by the merits. Doyle proves himself an energetic, entertaining, and knowledgeable photographer.

1   John Hill Burton would appear to have been the inspiration
for "Dr. Hill Barton", which is the name on the visiting card used
by Dr. Watson in "The Adventure of the Illustrious Client".
There is also a similarity between the title of *The Book Hunter*
and of Doyle's short story, "The Beetle Hunter".

2   Doyle makes a passing reference to the firm of Innes and
Burton in his short story, "Our Derby Sweepstakes", which was
published in *London Society* in May 1882. The heroine, Nelly
Montague, recalls how she had kept a fish which in time created
an insidious odour in the house and "caused mother to send an
abusive letter to Mr. Burton, who had pronounced our drainage
to be all that could be desired".

3   As well as using "Burton" for her daughter, Mary Doyle also
used the name "Innes" which she gave to her youngest son.

4   W.K. Burton died at 7 Itchome Nagata, Cho Kosimachi,
Tokyo, on 5 August 1899. In his will, which named John Milne
and Charles Dickenson West as executors, he bequeathed his
effects (valued at £638-3-3d) to his wife, Matsei, and asked that
she should "care for the female child named Tama as her daughter".

5   Silas K. Hocking, in an article in the *New Age* of 24 January
1895 called "A Holiday with Conan Doyle", describes Doyle's
photographic exploits during a visit to Switzerland in the summer
of 1893: "Doyle had brought a 'Kodak' with him, with a capacity
for about a hundred snapshots. I saw the results of his photographic skill later on in his house at Norwood . . . That 'Kodak'
came into use every day and in all sorts of places, and many of the
results were exceedingly good."

AFTER CORMORANTS WITH A CAMERA

It was about the end of July that my old friend "Chawles" dropped in upon me in Edinburgh. We always called him "Chawles" though no one could ever tell why, as his name is Thomas. Unshackled by a profession, and a keen shot, he is endeavouring to vary the humdrum monotony of ordinary sport, either by the discovery of some fresh game or by devising new means of circumventing the old. He disclosed his latest project amid clouds of tobacco smoke:- "The Isle of May, my boy! That's the place for this year! None of your tame rabbits and semi-civilised pheasants over there; but fine, old, pre-Adamite cormorants 'with a most ancient and fish-like smell.' That's where a fellow can knock the cobwebs out of him, Bob! By the way, old man," he continued, glancing at my camera and batch of printing-frames cooking in the sunshine, "why not come along? It's the very place for you. Think of the old black cliffs, the caves, the basalt, and all that sort of thing. Bring your filthy paraphernalia along with you. Start on Wednesday and we shall be back by Saturday night. Why not? Say 'yes' and it's a fixture."

Why not, indeed? The University session was over, my friends out of town, Princes-street a howling wilderness, and I in need of a change. The Isle of May seemed to offer "fresh fields and pastures new" both for myself and to my camera.

"Well, 'Chawles,' " I said, "if you won't drink my cyanide or 'fiddle' with my plate-carriers, and will promise to conduct yourself generally like a respectable christian, I'm your man."

"Done with you!" said "Chawles," reaching over his hand to ratify the bargain. "That is a fixture then."

"Couldn't we get another fellow?" said I. "We'd have room to quarrel then." Who could we get! This was a question easier to ask than to answer. There was Singleton, but he didn't drink; there was Jack Hawkins, but he drank too much; then there was

Holmes, but he neither smoked nor drank; while Godfrey's continual wails about his pipe were fatal to peace and quietness. Who should it be? "Happy thought!" said I. "Who d'ye think I met in town today? The Doctor! He is our man!"

This was carried *nem con.*, for no objection could be raised against the Doctor. His one fault of hatching vile puns and incubating over-abstruse riddles was rather agreeable than otherwise as offering a safety-valve for objurgations. In wet weather he was simply invaluable, being the proud possessor of a sepulchral bass and an unlimited stock of music-hall ditties. These considerations were duly weighed and "Chawles" despatched as an ambassador to the Doctor's hotel, while I took advantage of the last hours of sunlight to finish off my printing.

By the Tuesday evening everything had been arranged. "Chawles" came up to superintend the packing, which he did with his feet gracefully balanced upon the mantlepiece and a tumbler of toddy between them. The Doctor was there in great force, squatting like a toad in my arm chair, his beady eyes twinkling through a cloud of smoke, whence, like the Oracle of Delphi, he emitted an occasional word of wisdom.

I selected for the journey a folding, bellows-body, half-plate camera, by Meagher, with half-a-dozen double backs. These I had made according to the American plan, with the slides drawing entirely out. For all sizes up to and including whole plate I much prefer this arrangement to the usual one. My reasons for this are various. In the first place the slides are somewhat lighter; then, as they do not open in the centre, the chance of light being admitted is reduced to a minimum. I consider, too, that they are much easier to handle in a heavy wind; and, finally, their cost is only about two-thirds.

I had two stands – one a short ash tripod, the other an invention of my own, which I have found of great service in working the moorlands of Scotland. It simply consists of a stout walking-staff four feet long and shod with iron. This is fitted to the camera by means of an adjustable ball-and-socket joint. The advantages which I claim for this simple arrangement are not only its lightness (a consideration which will have weight with every practical worker in the open air) but also its cheapness, and the facility it affords for the focussing of a moving object. By it free movement is secured in every direction, both horizontal and vertical, while four inches of iron spike are sufficient to guarantee perfect steadiness.

I selected from among my lenses a single achromatic for ordinary use, and a rapid rectilinear with drop shutter for instantaneous work. The plates were of my own manufacture. They were made by the boiling method of our worthy chief Editor, and, being exquisitely sensitive, they enabled me to get many instantaneous exposures. As we intended that our trip should extend over several days, we took with us enough chemicals to develop a few plates after each day's work. To these I added, on the recommendation which appeared in THE BRITISH JOURNAL OF PHOTOGRAPHY, three ferrotype dishes – an innovation which the results of this tour have more than justified. We took with us also a policeman's lantern; but, as I omitted the small piece of ruby glass which I had intended to insert behind the lens, it was utterly useless as a dark-room light. We were enabled, however, to get over this difficulty at the cost of consuming the contents of a bottle labelled "hock," the taste of which forcibly reminded me of the day on which I accidentally gorged myself upon my clearing solution of citric acid and alum. We heated the end of the empty bottle and then dipped it into cold water, when the rapid contraction caused the bottom to fall out. A candle end placed under this afforded us a very satisfactory red light. I merely mention this little circumstance as a hint to your readers should they ever chance to be similarly circumstanced.

With these *impedimenta* carefully corded up in a strong deal box I felt myself equal to any photographic emergency. It was at this stage of the proceedings that the Doctor exhibited the first indications of his chronic infirmities. A gurgling in his throat and an apoplectic hue about his "gills" prepared us for the worst. "Why," he demanded, "is Bob's new stand like a cardsharper in Tripoli?" Let us draw a veil over the answer. Suffice it that the atrocity depended upon the fact that each was adapted for working upon a soft moor!

Wednesday morning found us on board the "Fiery Cross," bound for the goodly port of Anstruther. The weather was deliciously calm; not a breeze ruffled the surface of the water or the digestion of the passengers. "Chawles" paced the bridge in an Ulster capacious enough to envelope a small family, while the Doctor perched himself upon the forecastle, and amused himself by making hideous faces at a jaundiced infant, unseen by its unconscious parents.

Before us stretched the long line of the Fifeshire coast, while behind, wreathed in the morning mist, lay the modern Athens – Arthur's Seat, like a crouching lion, looming above the great sea of vapour. As the sun rose in the heavens, spire after spire and tier upon tier of houses pierced the pall that hid them from our view, and ere we had reached mid channel we could see the grim old city standing out sharp and clear against the morning sky. The steamboat was so steady that I could not resist the temptation of uncording the deal box, hauling my camera on deck, and trying the effects of a rapid exposure. A rugged mass of cumuli had piled themselves up behind the city. It was here that I first learned to appreciate a "dodge" communicated to me by my friend, Mr. W.K. Burton, which I now infinitely prefer to the sky-shade. The artifice is as simple as it is effective. Take a cabinet mount, and cut in it an aperture into which the cap of the lens will just fit; varnish the whole mount black. In lifting off the cap be careful to shade the lens by keeping the card horizontal. By this means beautiful cloud effects can be obtained, even in the most trying lights, though, of course, much depends upon the delicate manipulation and correct exposure. In this instance I estimate the exposure to have been, with the lens working about f 20, between one-half and three-quarters of a second. The resulting negative was certainly one of my very best.

Midday and a flowing tide took us into the little harbour of Anstruther. Shouldering my precious apparatus I summoned the reluctant Doctor from his bilious pot, and tore "Chawles" away from a fair one upon the bridge, whom he had enveloped in that wondrous garment of his. The wrench of parting told so heavily upon both my tender-hearted friends that they subsided into the bar of the "Anstruther Arms" and proceeded to drown their cares in the flowing bowl. How long they would have stopped is a matter of conjecture had not the arrival of the coach for Crail nipped them in the bud, and cut short a Platonic flirtation between "Chawles" and a barmaid of doubtful attractions. The Doctor ascended the coach, *riddling* the place with conundrums, to use his own expression. They were for the most part too nauseous for repetition. Staring vacantly at the cap of our buxom landlady, he was understood to mutter that it was really too "mutch" – a joke which met with no encouragement and pined away in its early infancy.

A smart four-mile drive, varied by occasional glimpses of the German Ocean, brought us to the ancient and honourable Burgh of Crail. The coachman drew up his smoking steeds in front of the "Golf Inn," and one by one we alighted from our perches. The quaint little hostelry looked pre-eminently homely and comfortable, while a savoury smell of beefsteaks and onions from a kitchen door left artfully ajar whetted an appetite already painfully keen. Dinner was speedily ordered, and in the interval of its preparation "Chawles" and I decided upon having "a dip," leaving the Doctor extended upon the solitary sofa. Passing down the main street, which, to quote Mark Twain, is "not quite as straight as a rainbow nor as crooked as a corkscrew" (a merciful dispensation of Providence to a not too sober population), we headed for the beach. There, apparently less than half its real distance from the land, lay the island which was the goal of our expedition. We both gazed at its basalt cliffs, flecked with white, but with very different sentiments.

"Think what might be done by two guns in a boat," I heard "Chawles" mutter, while my own ruling feeling was one of regret that I had not done better justice to its varied scenery by bringing another dozen of plates.

We finished our bathe and started back to the hotel, where we found our Æsculapius with an injured look on his face and a watch like a warming-pan in his hand. He was singing "Dinna forget" in an aggrieved minor key, as a delicate allusion to our want of punctuality, while he sniffed the fragrance from a brace of roast fowls which had just been served up from the kitchen. We did ample justice to really excellent cookery; and after dinner, with a glass of toddy under our belts to assist digestive powers, we mutually agreed that there were worse places for the tired way-farer than the comfortable parlour of the "Golf Inn."

We retired early to "roost" as it had been settled that we were to sail for the May early the following morning. Before "turning in" I took the opportunity of the darkness to transfer a dozen plates to my carriers. For an hour or two I was kept awake by a nasal duet, in which "Chawles" produced a fine chromatic effect by snoring baritone to the Doctor's bass. Gradually, however, I dropped off into troubled slumbers broken by the repeated asseverations of a reveller in the street below that he "was na' fou', he was na' fou'" – an assertion which he was endeavouring to prove by arguments to the solitary lamp-post of the Burgh.

At about six in the morning an inarticulate howl from a slip-shod chambermaid summoned us regretfully from our beds. We dressed rapidly, and each made his own preparations for the task before him. "Chawles" extracted from its case a "double ten" by Greener, whose shining barrels and polished stock would hardly lead one to suppose how many brace of birds had gone down before it. The Doctor put in an appearance at breakfast, armed with a gigantic piece of ordnance which some confiding gunsmith had entrusted to him in a moment of weakness.

"None of your patent dodges here," said he. "Give me the infant, four drachms of powder, and a handful of 'double B,' and I'm contented. No bird will cross the field of this single achro-matic, double combination, instantaneous triplet without my getting the focus of it. Eh, old boy?" and he gave me a playful dig in the ribs. I afterwards found that our medical friend had been industriously perusing the advertising pages of my copy of THE BRITISH JOURNAL PHOTOGRAPHIC ALMANAC, which accounted for this sudden effervescence of technicalities.

Porridge and milk, ham and eggs, coffee and chalkless cream went down before us, and we sallied forth from the hotel well primed for the work of the day. Arriving at the harbour we were greeted by a grizzly and splay-footed mariner, old enough, apparently, to be the father of Coleridge's hero. "Here she is, sir!" he bellowed, leading us along the quay to a little craft which was moored beside the jetty. Another sailor, more grizzly and splay-footed than the last, was busily engaged in casting off the moorings. A suspicious smell of the wine of the country and a roll in their gait told us that even at that early hour they had been partaking of something stronger than zoedone. "Shove her out, Sinbad!" said the Doctor, grounding arms upon the toe of our original friend by way of attracting his attention.

"Hech! man," I heard that worthy grumble to his mate, while he thoughtfully rubbed his injured extremity, "yon's an awfu' mannie – the chiel wi' the muckle gun!" They spread the brown sail in a trice, and as it bellied to the northerly breeze we shot out of the little harbour.

The weather was of that clear, breezy character which warms the heart of a photographer. Our light craft danced like a cork upon a heavy swell setting up channel from the North Sea, and "Chawles" began audibly to regret that final plate of porridge. The Doctor seemed impervious to the nauseating influence. He was apparently too busy gauging the mental capacity of our Palinurus.

"Never been out of Crail?" he asked.

"Ou, aye! mony's the time. I've been tae Cockanzie and ance to Farfar."

"Splendid town that!" said the Doctor, with a nod towards the little knot of houses astern, and a wink which was wasted upon the bilious "Chawles."

"Aye, a braw toun," quoth Sinbad, with native pride.

"You must be lively in the winter time," said the seductive physician.

"Aye, an' an awfu' wicked place," assented the veteran, with a leer of much meaning.

"Lots of dissipation, I suppose," suggested the Doctor.

"Folks wha hae na lived here can form na idea o't."

"What sort of dissipation?" I asked.

"A' sorts of dissipation," answered the vaguely-comprehensive *roué*; and, having invested his native village with this lurid and gloomy interest, he playfully expectorated upon the prostrate "Chawles," and proceeded to haul down the sheet as we glided into the little rocky cove which served as a harbour to the Isle of May.

It had been arranged that we were to commence operations upon the cliffs. As there are no inhabitants upon the island, except the keepers of the lighthouse, we had only our own convenience to consult. Springing ashore we made our way up the rough pathway which leads past the lighthouse. It was here that I got my first plate, including the rocky cliff and the boat lying snugly moored among the rocks below. A second, and a very successful one, I got from a grassy knoll a few hundred yards further inland. The brightness of the morning sun compelled me to adopt the precaution for shading which I have already described. The subject was a difficult one to treat, the hard, white outlines of the lighthouse tending to produce that photographic abomination best described as "chalk and charcoal." I separated the plate, however, from the rest, and by reducing the amount of pyro. in the developer I was enabled ultimately to obtain a harmonious picture.

Meanwhile the sportsmen had got well to work, and were making havoc among the sea birds as they rose in myriads from the caves below.

"Chawles," now completely himself again, was scientifically disposing of something like a brace a minute, while every now and then a crash like a small cannon proclaimed that the Doctor's muzzle-loader was "under weigh," his victims being easily recognised by their shattered appearance. "Have a crack at them, Bob," he said, offering me his gun, but I explained to him that my shoulder joint was valuable to me, and that I had no wish to have it dislocated. He took a horrible revenge upon me for my refusal by digging a gristly riddle out of his mind and hurling it at me. "Why is the lighthouse-keeper like Lord Cardigan?" he asked. "Because he is one of the light brigade, of course," and he gave a guffaw which raised quite a cloud of birds, while I hurried away with my camera before he could fabricate another.

On coming down to the beach on the southern side of the island a beautiful spectacle met my eyes. Nine fine yachts of the Forth Club were rounding the point of the island, each under a cloud of canvas and lying well over, for the breeze was beginning to freshen. They looked like some great flock of sea birds as they rose and fell on the crests of the waves. The appearance of these tempted me to bring out my own patent stand and fix to my camera the rapid lens and shutter. The light was exceedingly brilliant. I reduced the aperture to about f 1/3. The distance of the nearest yacht was such that the lens being focussed for "the distance" did not require to be further adjusted. I took care that the iron spike was driven deep in the sand, so as to ensure steadiness. After once fixing the camera I did not use the focussing glass, but trusted to my eye to judge when the yacht would cross the axis of the lens. My shutter gives what an unscientific friend of mine calls a "long instantaneous exposure;" that is to say, from an eighth to a tenth of a second, which I consider short enough for almost any purpose.

Let me take this opportunity of laying great stress upon the advantage of having the aperture in the shutter several times the diameter of the lens in the direction in which the shutter moves. If this be not attended to the effect is practically, for a given length of exposure, to reduce the amount of light which reaches the plates, without the advantages which would result by bringing about the same reduction of light by the use of a smaller diaphragm. In this case every plate out of the half-dozen we exposed received a proper actinic impression.

By this time it was nearly two o'clock, and the picture of the lunch basket which we had left in the sheets of the boat began to rise lovingly before my mind. There was no difficulty in rejoining my companions, as their shots and shouts were audible all over the island. I toiled up the hill with my camera and found them in a little valley beyond. They seemed surfeited with slaughter, and hailed the idea of lunch with enthusiasm.

"Not a bad morning's work," said "Chawles," triumphantly. "Forty-three cormorants, nine rock pigeons, two mallets, a curlew, and a bo'sun gull – pretty good for two guns!"

"Sinbad was to bring up the basket at half-past one, wasn't he?" I asked.

"Yes; confound him!" growled the Doctor, "it's close on two now. You fellows wait here and I'll go and hurry him up."

"Well, look sharp!" said we, so dropping his gun and a bad joke, the Doctor passed over the brow of the hill and disappeared. He was away about ten minutes when he returned without the basket, but in a state of excitement.

"Come after me, Bob!" he said, his little black eyes dancing with mischief. "Bring your camera and come quick." With these words he led the way down a hill and through some furze bushes. "Now, quietly!" he whispered, as we crawled up to a large boulder.

"Look over that and don't speak."

I raised my head slowly over the rock, but it was all I could do to fulfil the latter portion of his precept. There, not fifteen yards off, sat Sinbad with our luncheon basket open before him. At that particular moment he had just emptied a third of our whisky bottle down his throat, and was bending down at the little spring while he filled it up again with water.

"Look sharp!" whispered the Doctor. "Take him before he sees you!" We raised the camera.

I rapidly and noiselessly made the necessary preparations and the *roué* was taken in the act.

"That's a pretty conclusive bit of evidence," said the Doctor, as we quietly went back as we had come. "We'll keep it up as a little surprise for him. The son of a seacook! to go and water our grog! Now we are far enough off and out of sight. Hollo! Hollo! Sinbad!"

"I'm comin'," said a voice, and the mariner appeared from behind the rock, staggering along under the weight of the basket.

"Come on, man!" cried the Doctor. "You are as slow as promotion in the navy."

"I'm gey sorry to ha' kept ye waitin', but my banes are getting unco'auld," explained Sinbad. "Ablins' I'm as weel as ony ither mon o' my age."

"You've not been drinking anything out of the basket, have you?" said I sternly. The *roué* drew himself up. There was all the conscious pride of innocence in every feature of his face, albeit you could smell his breath at the distance of ten yards. He put his gnarled old hand upon his breast:-

"Maybe ye dinna' ken," he said, "that I'm an elder o' the free kirk o' Scotland." There was a wealth of humour in the way in which the old sinner rolled out this clinching piece of evidence.

"By jove!" said the Doctor, "I feel that we have acted brutally towards him. There are depths in Sinbad which we have not fathomed as yet. I declare I won't be sure he did do it till that photograph is developed."

We felt that the accusation should not be pressed as yet, so we endeavoured to repair the veteran's injured feelings by giving him a help with the basket, which we conveyed to the spot where "Chawles" was waiting. Here we seated ourselves, and, looking down at the golden sand and the quiet blue expanse stretching away to the horizon, we agreed that no king on earth had a dining-hall like ours. It was a jovial meal, and when we wound up on a glass of grog, and the Doctor obliged the company with "The Midshipmite" in a charnel-house voice, even Sinbad's old grim face relaxed, and he was understood to express his forgiveness of all injuries received at the hands of the singer.

After luncheon the sportsmen went back to their birds, and I wandered off over the island, getting two more very fine side views of the great caves, ribbed in with their basaltic columns. I then walked over to the lighthouse and made arrangements with the keeper for putting us up that night, as we did not intend to take the boat back until the afternoon of the next day. Having made this all right I worked round again towards the sportsmen. It was at this time that the idea of a photographic novelty occurred to me – why not take a cormorant at the moment of its being shot? I had a few plates to spare, so that at the worst no harm would be done. "Chawles" entered into the idea most enthusiastically.

"This is the place for your camera," he said, glancing along the line of cliffs with a sportsman's eye, and pointing to a slight promontory which overlooked the sea. "You run your spike into the grass there, and I'll stand a little to the side of you and shoot everything that passes in front of you."

I fixed the camera in the place selected and focussed for "the distance" as before. The method of further procedure was to adjust the shutter, to place the plate in position, withdraw the slide, and follow the motion of the flying bird as accurately as possible by hand. When I heard the report of the gun I was to "fire away." The first three, we were almost certain, were failures, as the birds were flying directly across the field of the lens. In the fourth case the bird was coming straight towards us, and we had every reason to believe that it would be a success. We could not afford to waste another plate, and we contented ourselves with this one, of which more anon.

By this time, as the light was not quite so good as it had been, I thought I should have a relaxation from my labours, so leaving my camera I borrowed the keeper's boat and deep sea line, and put off about a hundred yards from the shore. Here, with some fresh sprats for bait and my pipe for company, I spent a most luxurious evening, the calm of which was only varied by the occasional sight of the Doctor aiming at some bird between himself and the boat. I was out an hour and a half, and had nearly as good sport as my companions, for I got a dozen gurnard, four bream, a ling, a hake, and a rock cod.

We dined luxuriously at the lighthouse upon a bream and a leg of mutton, which the worthy keeper had stored up for his Sunday dinner. Indeed, nothing could exceed the hospitality of these good people, who were evidently delighted at the unusual sight of a new face. The wife gave a long and dismal account of a stout Frenchman who had come over for some shooting, and had put a charge of shot into the leg of the eldest son. The Doctor, in his official capacity, was taken up and dressed the wound, which he pronounced to be doing well. Even the atmosphere of the sick room could not cure his irresistible propensity, for he asked me, with many chuckles, what was the difference between that Frenchman and some of my chemicals, the answer being, I believe, that "the one was a Gallic fully developed, and the other a full pyrogallic developer!"

There was great excitement in the evening over the development of the dying cormorant, and a nasty accident nearly ruined it. We were peering over each other's shoulders breathlessly watching "the detail coming up," when the Doctor, by some unlucky mischance, knocked over the hock bottle. The plate was only saved by my presence of mind in extinguishing the candle, judging the time requisite to complete the development, and flooding the plate with water in the dark. To my delight and, I must add, to my great surprise the plate was eventually a complete success. The bird came out as "sharp as a die," and even several stray feathers floating around it could be distinctly made out. The loss of the hock bottle ended our developing for that tour. Luckily, before its decline and fall we had finished off the plate of Sinbad in the act of watering our whisky. The others could wait, as we had determined to be in Edinburgh again by next evening.

The weather next morning was certainly not calculated to make us prolong our stay. There was a heavy Scotch mist, and a thin drizzle of rain which soaked through an Ulster far more rapidly than an ostentatious downpour. Sport and photography were alike out of the question. It was then that the Doctor showed the stuff that was in him. He cheered us with song after song and depressed us with riddle after riddle, so that the time passed wonderfully until Sinbad looked in and announced that the tide was right for sailing. We bade adieu to our worthy friends in the lighthouse; and, having got my implements and specimens from the game bag aboard, we shoved our little craft off, and another hour saw us once more in the dissipated town of Crail. We made for our former quarters at the "Golf Inn," and after drying ourselves and having some refreshments proceeded to take our places in the Anstruther coach. Old Sinbad had come up to see us off.

Just as the horses were starting the Doctor gravely said – "Sinbad, we are sorry even for a moment to have suspected an elder of the church of such a crime as theft. We think some apology is due to you, and you will find it inside this packet." So saying, he solemnly handed him a little parcel containing a print of the old sailor as he appeared when industriously pouring water into the whisky bottle. The driver cracked his whip and we shot away along the country road; but the last we saw of Crail was old Sinbad, too much horrified to speak, glaring at the dumb accuser before him.

Our home journey was as pleasant as the rest of the trip, and we were back in Edinburgh by seven o'clock. That our little excursion was a social success and thoroughly enjoyable from beginning to end may be seen even by this bald description. Photographically, in spite of the abominable weather of the second day, it was far from being a failure. Out of the two dozen plates we were enabled to show a dozen and a half negatives, of which no photographer need have been ashamed – a result which, I consider, working under such exceptional circumstances, would be wellnigh unattainable by the wet process. They showed every gradation from clear glass in the shadows to photographic opacity in the high lights.

I am very sure that my companions stowed away their guns with the same resolution which I formed as I stacked my camera in the old corner, namely, that a year should not elapse without renewing our acquaintance with our friends, the cormorants.

ON THE SLAVE COAST WITH A CAMERA

—◆—

I do not suppose that there is any reader of THE BRITISH JOURNAL OF PHOTOGRAPHY who is meditating a journey to the West Coast of Africa.

If such there be, and he has any option in the matter, let me impress upon him *Punch's* time-honoured advice before matrimony – "Don't." Should it happen, however, that the force of circumstances is too strong for him, and that he is fain to go, he has my profound sympathy, and the cheering assurance that at least one of the cameriferous brotherhood has trod the path before him.

It was with a light heart that I packed up my boxes about the middle of October, and set out for Liverpool to join my vessel. There was a charm about the great list of ports at which we were advertised to call – Madeira, Teneriffe, Canary, Sierra Leone, Monrovia, Cape Coast Castle, Bonny, Lagos, Old Calabar, and a score of others, whose very names had been hitherto unknown to me. I had a beatific vision of strange negatives. The luxuriant growth of the African forest; the haughty grace of the untamed savage as he trod his native wilderness, or yearned in his simple untutored way for a slice out of the calf of your leg; the mighty rivers and the cloud-capped mountains – all these should be transferred to the tell-tale paper and be a record among countless generations yet unborn of the adventurous spirit of their ancestors. Such were a few of my milder aspirations as I stowed away my chemicals in the old deal box, and got together all the other photographic apparatus necessary for a lengthy campaign.

The voyage was to extend over rather more than three months, and the important question now arose as to what was to be taken and how much of each. I knew that everything there was any possibility of my needing must go with me, as I was informed that there was no town on the coast where decent gunpowder, to say nothing of such refinements as photographic necessities, could be obtained. It may be of interest to some other unfortunate wanderer to know the conclusions at which I arrived, and how far they were justified by my subsequent experience.

My camera was my old favourite – a folding bellows-body half-plate, by Meagher, with double swing back. As I have already mentioned incidentally in THE BRITISH JOURNAL OF PHOTO-GRAPHY, I much prefer those made upon the American principle, with the slides drawing entirely out. This holds good for all sizes up to and including full plate. There are many and very varied reasons for this opinion. They are lighter, less expensive, less liable to admit light owing to the fact of their not opening in the centre, and, finally, are far more easy to manage when there is any wind. The latter may seem rather a fanciful advantage at first sight, but I can recall instances in my own modest photographic career where great events hung upon this single fact, and I have little doubt that other readers of the Journal who have had much experience of outdoor working can corroborate me in what I say.

I took a stout ash tripod and also one of my own invention, which has already been described in the Journal. It simply consists of a single stout stick, fitted with a strong iron spike and a ball-and-socket joint. The difference of weight I have found to be no small consideration in a climate which is hot enough to render the weight of a napkin upon your knee at dinner time utterly unbearable.

The lenses which I took were the following:- First, a wide-angle "landscape" lens, which I used whenever I could, always bearing in mind that this form is comparatively slow and the angle limited. I find that the so-called "single" lens gives, *cæteris paribus*, a more brilliant picture than is given by any other. Secondly, I took a "symmetrical," to be used where a large angle was desirable. Thirdly, a "rapid rectilinear" of long focus, which would come useful where instantaneous effects were needed, as also in groups or portraits. I took no "portrait" lens, as with modern dry plates and the brilliant tropical sunlight I consider such to be quite unnecessary. I also took a drop shutter of the simplest possible description I had had made for me before leaving Liverpool, a leather case with compartments, into which each of the items mentioned above (always excepting the stand) fitted accurately, so that I could carry them readily across country.

I must admit that one of my leading photographic faults hitherto has been a certain impetuosity, which has led me to prefer developing upon the spot to waiting until I had the con-veniences of my laboratory around me. In spite of the precedent

of Colonel Stuart Wortley and various others who have photographed in tropical regions, and, as I understand, brought their
plates home for the purpose of development, I determined in this
case also to attempt it as I went along. This being my resolution, I
found it necessary to take with me chemicals sufficient to develop
not only occasional test plates but my whole series. I may mention
incidentally, and in my own excuse, that my experience has led
me to believe that the latent image in gelatine plates actually fades
to such an extent that a far different result is got if plates be
developed within a few days of exposure from what would be
brought about if they were kept for some months.

I have always been a strong advocate for alkaline pyro.
development. I therefore took the chemicals necessary for this
form with me, namely, pyrogallic acid, strong ammonia, and
bromide of ammonium. I trusted to the medicine chest for the
citric acid to mix up this developer.

And here I may mention the first of my shortcomings as a
warning to such readers as "go down to the sea in ships" and take
their cameras with them. I had taken a pint stoppered bottle of
strong ammonia, which I kept in my berth with my other chemicals. Shortly after our arrival in tropical regions a strong pungent
smell warned me of some casualty, and on examination I found
that the stopper had been blown out of the bottle, owing, no
doubt, to the great heat, and that the fluid had all escaped. There
was not a dry eye at dinner that evening. As the captain remarked,
paraphrasing Tom Moore – "You may scowl at the surgeon, and
swear if you will, but the smell of his hartshorn will hang round
you still." After this I was compelled to use washing soda as an
alkali. I think, however, that upon the whole the results were
quite as good as those afforded by ammonia.

Another piece of advice in travelling is never to take anything
for granted. I had trusted to the medical department for a plentiful supply of spirits of wine to use for drying negatives and
various other purposes. I found, however, after leaving Liverpool, that the ship was poorly provided in this respect. When the
temperature was very high I was much annoyed by the tendency
of negatives to "run," and found the want of spirit a very great
drawback.

As regards the plates themselves, I should say that, as I had not
had time to prepare them myself, I took nothing but commercial
ones – in all twelve dozen.

I used the bath-room of the ship as a substitute for a dark-
room, and by closing the port with a towel, and using one of the
ship's lanterns wrapped completely in red Turkey cloth, I suc-

ceeded in extemporising a little "den," which answered every purpose wonderfully well. I found developing trays made of ebonite to be both the cheapest and the best owing to their combined lightness and toughness.

I had a great desire to "astonish the natives" by representations of their own hideous faces. I therefore took printing materials along with me, which included three light frames, some toning material, and ready-sensitised paper. The latter I cut to the size to be used, and kept in one of the printing-frames wrapped in waterproof cloth. It speaks well for the perfection to which the manufacture of this paper has been brought that a large piece in my possession, which has travelled the whole way to Africa and back, is still perfectly white.

I was delighted to find, on arriving at Liverpool, that one of my brother officers was an old schoolfellow – as good a fellow as ever breathed, and an enthusiastic disciple of gelatine. He is one of those photographic fanatics whose first impulse, if charged by a mad dog, would be to focus it, and his second to take to his heels. He was sitting on the poop, when I came aboard, on a box which might have been the twin brother of my own, with a venerable-looking camera propped up against the rail beside him, and in his enthusiasm at meeting me he very nearly succeeded in pushing the companion of his labours into the muddy waters of the dock. We got the ill-used veteran upon his legs again, however, with no greater injury than the loss of a little varnish, and we proceeded conjointly to stow away our apparatus in a place of safety.

It was as well that we got it comfortably down among the lumber, for immediately after leaving the Mersey we found ourselves in the middle of a terrible hurricane. To quote an old Scotch song – "It blew a most awfu' blow." We passed down the Irish Sea and into the channel, steaming before the wind in a fog so thick that it was hardly possible to see a wave before it came crashing in a green wall over our bulwarks. Had we but known it, the ill-fated "Clan Macduff" must at one time have been close beside us, but, even had we seen it, any attempt at a rescue would have been fruitless in such a sea. It was not until our third day out, when we were fairly in the Bay of Biscay, that the wind began to moderate, and that some appearance of order was restored among our goods and chattels. My own cabin had been flooded by a wave, but I was too busy attending to the prostrate ladies to have time to think about my own woes. As the sky cleared, however, and the angry sea changed into a long, greasy swell, there was a gradual divorce between our passengers and the basins. One of them even had the hardihood to appear upon deck with a sickly look of confidence upon his face, which, I regret to state, suddenly faded away, to give place to an earnest and all-absorbing interest in the appearance of the water alongside of the vessel.

"After all," said another – a clergyman of scientific proclivities, as he found himself getting over his ailments – "the sea is a very paltry thing when you come to think of it – only an endless repetition of two molecules of hydrogen with one of oxygen, and some salts in suspension. There's nothing very dignified about that. I have no reverence for the ocean." I was about to remark that the ocean seemed to have precious little reverence for him, but he was called away at this moment by pressing business at one of the port-holes.

After a week's pitching and tossing we made the rugged island of Porto Sancto inhabited by a few scattered fishermen and collectors of seaweed. Here, encouraged by the steadiness of the ship, my friend Tom and I began operations, and with very fair success. We had a most enjoyable little run ashore next morning at Funchal, the capital of Madeira, obtaining several excellent little "bits" and characteristic groups. Our best result was a photograph of the town, done from the sea-side with a very wide-angle lens in the evening. We found that the soft light of the setting sun was better adapted for good work than the midday glare, as the whitewashed houses tend to produce a very chalky effect. This tendency to chalkiness caused me much mental perturbation in all the tropical views which included anything in the shape of a house. It was only by reducing the strength of the developer that I was enabled to obtain harmonious pictures, and even then some were sadly marred by the hard, white effects. We were unfortunate that day in other ways, as a misunderstanding as to who was to regulate the requisite exposure very nearly ruined one of our finest plates.

Leaving Madeira behind us, we got into the trade winds, and found ourselves within thirty-six hours lying abreast of Vera Cruz, the capital of Teneriffe. I regret to say that, though we had a momentary glimpse of the Peak, it became clouded over with mist, and we were unable to add it to our little series. We got capital views of some of the lesser mountains, however, and of the quaint little town itself, with its cathedral and frowning batteries. It was these batteries which had the honour of inflicting upon our immortal Nelson the only defeat he ever sustained, and in the cathedral the ensign captured from him on that occasion used to be hung. A midshipman came ashore, however, some years ago from a British man-of-war, and managed to break into the cathedral and carry off the flag. What became of the young reefer

I know not, though rumour says dismissal from the service was the reward of his ill-judged patriotism.

After touching at Canary we pursued our way to Sierra Leone. This was the most pleasant part of our voyage, steaming steadily for seven days through a lonely and unruffled sea. It is true that there was no variety to charm the eye of the photographer, yet it was pleasant to lie under the awnings in the cool of the evening, watching the flying fish as they flickered, like bars of silver, over the crests of the waves. When the moon came out, too, our ladies used to be enticed upon deck, the music and songs would while away the time. The only blot which I can remember upon the peacefulness of this life was a vile proposal from my brother artist that he and I should sing "The March of the Camera Men" – a remark which I regarded as a jocular curiosity, and am willing to back for imbecility against any utterance of modern times.

Sierra Leone – cheerfully designated "The White Man's Grave" – is situated on the bed of a river about five miles from the sea. As we lay in front of the town a whole fleet of canoes passed us having aboard some negro chieftain of eminence, as was indicated by the shouts of the rowers and the beating of the drums. The appearance of this flotilla induced me to fix to my camera the rapid lens and shutter. Under the combined influence of current and paddles they were passing very rapidly. They were so far away that the lens, having been focussed for the "distance," did not require to be altered. In such cases I never use the focussing glass, but trusted to my eye to inform me when the nearest canoe was crossing the axis of the lens. Let me here once again lay stress upon having the aperture in the shutter several times the diameter of the lens in the direction in which the shutter moves, otherwise the amount of light which reaches the plate is practically reduced, without the advantages resulting from the same reduction of light if caused by a smaller diaphragm. In this particular instance one plate was a failure, but three others were all fairly successful.

It would probably weary my readers to hear of our uneventful cruise down that fever-haunted coast. Many of our men were struck down by the miasma, and for some weeks the quinine bottle was more familiar to me than the developing tray. Passing the model colony of Liberia – pompously called "The New States" – and flying the American flag with one star in the corner, we rounded Cape Palmas and steamed down what may be fairly called, "The Cannibal Coast," it we may believe the accounts of the natives given by those who know them best and have had most opportunities of studying their customs. A great deal has been said about the regeneration of our black brothers and the latent virtues of the swarthy races. My own experience is that you abhor them on first meeting them, and gradually learn to dislike them a very great deal more as you become better acquainted with them. In spite of the epidemic of sickness which broke out among us, I succeeded in getting photographs of many of the men of light and leading among these interesting and primitive races. The majority of them are depicted as, to quote Mark Twain, wearing a smile and nothing more. I have one, however, resplendent in all the glory of a plug hat and umbrella. The rest of his clothing, however, he had apparently left behind in the family wardrobe!

A rather amusing incident occurred at Accra, which was our first important port after leaving Cape Coast Castle. A large canoe full of negroes happened to be engaged fishing within twenty yards of the ship, as she lay at her anchorage. I thought the opportunity of getting a characteristic and lifelike group too good to be neglected. I therefore got up my camera and was engaged focussing them, when, to my astonishment they gave a united yell and sprang overboard. The effect of the row of woolly heads glaring at me from the other side of the boat was so ludicrous that I attempted to make good use of the opportunity and expended a plate upon the group. I am sorry to say, however, that the results exhibited little better than a chaotic mass of white foam, distorted faces, and waving paddles, hardly distinguishable from each other. I then hailed them and asked what was the matter. "Me know dem thing," shouted one of them. "Me serve in man-o'-war. Dem thing gatling gun – all same Queen's ship have in tops. What you want point him at poor nigger for?" It was only when I had carried off the obnoxious instrument that the unfortunate fishermen could be persuaded to creep into their boat once more.

At Lagos I was myself knocked over with the fever, and was for several days in a semi-delirious condition. I am blessed, however, with a strong constitution, and before reaching Bonny, at the mouth of the Niger, I was able to crawl upon deck – very weak, it is true, but otherwise none the worse for what was undoubtedly a dangerous attack.

I had an opportunity, while at Bonny, of photographing one of the great war-chiefs, Wawirra by name – a sort of African Duke of Cambridge. He informed us that in his last campaign he had taken five hundred men. I remarked that I could "take" as many as that in a single moment. This small joke had to be explained to him at great length, until it gradually lost what little fun there was originally in it, and struck me as being about the most dismal piece of pleasantry that had ever been perpetrated. In spite of my frantic efforts I am convinced that that African left the ship with the deeply-rooted impression that I was a blood-curdling warrior, and was consumed by a chronic thirst for human gore! I afterwards learned that, in spite of his high position and ferocious exterior, he was a poor fighter himself – "too full of pluck to stand up," as my informant expressed it, so he lies at the bottom of the canoe and does the heavy work and the shouting.

Another very successful photograph was taken a little further down the coast, where we fell in with a British gunboat. She was steaming about eight knots at the time, and crossed our bows at a distance of a hundred and fifty yards. She came out wonderfully well, the ripple of the water and the faces of the man at the wheel and the officer on the bridge being, all things considered, remarkably distinct.

Fernando Po was our next port, and here again I was enabled to secure something which I flatter myself was a photographic novelty, namely, the picture of a large shark as it cruised about close to the surface of the water. These tigers of the sea are as numerous as flies on some parts of the African coast. If you drop anything with a splash into the water you will see far down on the confines of the realms of eternal darkness a horrible shadow appear, and this will come flickering up, developing a fin here and a patch of colour there; then you will see a cruel green eye looking up at you out of the water, and you will know that you have seen the Devil, or as near an approach to him as is to be found in this world. After photographing my friend I had the ingratitude to put a bullet through his dorsal fin, which seemed to astonish him considerably; for, after a wobble to express his opinion of the unwarrantable liberty I taken with him, he dived under the ship and disappeared.

Another interesting picture which I secured was that of the interior of one of the old slave barracoons, with the iron rings and fetters still riveted to the walls. In these horrible caves, dug out of the rock, hundreds of unfortunate negroes – men, women, and children – used to be packed pending the arrival of the slaver. From what I saw of them I should think that, when full of their struggling, thirsty occupants, the Black Hole of Calcutta would be a sanatorium by comparison.

Leaving Fernando Po we arrived at Old Calabar – a British colony situated sixty miles up the Calabar River. This was the turning point in our voyage, and we lay in the river for nearly a week, getting cargo aboard. While here I had several very interesting little runs up the stream, the photographic results of which I hope to dwell upon in a separate communication.

I had the privilege, while at Duke Town, of taking the portrait of a native prince. His highness did me the honour of informing me that it was wonderfully unlike him. The delight of his retinue, however, at seeing the ugliness of their lord so faithfully represented more than assuaged my wounded photographic feelings. It was an excellent likeness; but the monarch probably missed the smell of premature putridity which was so characteristic of the original, and yet could not be transferred to paper.

On our way up the coast we touched once again at the ports which we had already visited, and several interesting scenes that had been passed over through accident or press of work were now taken. The accursed fever broke out among us again, however, and one of our crew succumbed to it on Christmas Eve, and was buried at sea.

I fear that I have prolonged this little sketch to most unreasonable length. There were few incidents worth recording upon our homeward journey, until after we left Madeira. The Peak of Teneriffe was once again shrouded in vapour, and avoided our ever-watchful lenses.

After leaving Madeira we had a little temporary excitement, owing to the ship taking fire. The cause of it was unknown, but the mischief lay at the bottom of one of the great coal bunkers. It seemed a serious matter, as the greater part of our cargo consisted of palm oil. We hoped at first that it would smoulder until our arrival in Liverpool, but by the third morning matters looked so threatening that energetic measures had to be taken. All hands were called, and as many men as would fit sent below to move the coal, while the rest hoisted up the buckets from below. I took a photograph of this deck at this time, but such was the coolness and discipline aboard that no one looking casually at the picture would guess that anything was amiss. Four ominous streams of smoke, however, from the bunker-ventilators, disclose to a nautical eye the great danger in which the vessel lay. After twenty-four hours' anxiety, however, we were able to get the fire under, and the weary and exhausted crew were permitted to take a much-needed rest. The remainder of our voyage was devoid of interest, and the 14th of January found us once again in the docks of Liverpool.

This three months' voyage may, I think, be fairly called a photographic success. Both my fellow-worker and myself obtained a series of characteristic and picturesque effects which will be of interest to us for all our lives. The tendency to hardness and failure in giving idea of distance which I have already mentioned, and which is common to all tropical or semi-tropical views, is the only fault which I can find with them. I have already given it as my opinion that for general results gelatine is superior to any process which has gone before it. I have come to the conclusion, also, that the hardness to which I have just referred makes itself less evident when this process is used than with any other.

These artistic results, however, have been obtained at considerable risk to our health, and even to our lives. There is one advantage which I can confidently ascribe to the West Coast of Africa, and that is that after once visiting it there is no spot so barren that it does not seem luxurious in comparison. The laureate sings –

"Better fifty years of Europe than a cycle of Cathay,"

and I cordially endorse the sentiment. Better a week in the Welsh mountains with a light camera and a good companion than all the lights and shades of fever-haunted gorilla-land.

UP AN AFRICAN RIVER WITH THE CAMERA

———◆———

"Bang!" goes the signal gun, and the anchor drops with a dull slush into the slow-flowing stream, sending a fountain of thick, peasoup-coloured water and yellow spray into the air. The ship swings round at her moorings, and we find ourselves opposite the straggling settlement of Old Calabar.

It is not an imposing place to look at, though to the African mind, for many a hundred miles up and down the coast, it represents the commercial capital and the centre of all that is gay and dissipated.

Looking at it from the deck of the good ship "Syria," we see a muddy beach covered with canoes, one or two white factories facing the water, a background of miserable huts, and two larger zinc-roofed buildings which surmount the whole, one being the king's palace and the other the church – not by any means the place that one would go to in search of pleasure; but it is the outlet for the oil of a large area of palm-covered country, and the only port of importance between Bonny and Gaboon, so that to a commercial steamer like our own there are inducements to crawl up that sixty miles of shallow, dangerous river, with the branches snapping against the yards of the ship and the lead going without intermission on both sides of the vessel. We can already see the great casks of oil lying littered about beside the crumbling wharfs, which show us that our journey has not been made in vain.

I am busily engaged bringing my wide-angle lens to bear upon the scene, and trying to tone down the glare by a temporary awning, when the Captain comes along cheerily rubbing his hands.

"Seventy forty-inch puncheons if there's one, Doctor!" said he; "but it's one of their confounded saint's days or Eboe days, or whatever they call them, and they won't do a stroke of work till tomorrow. What shall we do this evening?"

"Well," I said, "I think the best thing I can do is to get a negative or two ashore."

"Bother that camera of yours!" says the skipper, shaking his fist at my trusty old folding bellows-body, half-plate, by Meagher. "Can't you be sociable just for once in a way?"

"Well, what do you propose?"

"Anything that is lively. Here's Haines, the purser. We'll get his opinion. Here, Haines!"

"Well?" said Haines, with a grin of anticipation upon his rubicund countenance.

"Here's the Doctor wants to spend his evening with his head in a bag, glaring through a little round hole. What are we to do with him?"

"Take him a cruise up the river."

"*Chacun à son gout*," I remark, with an attempt at dignity.

"Everybody has the gout," the Captain translated with flippancy.

"Look here; we'll have a compromise. We'll start up the river when it gets cooler, and the Doctor shall have the bows of the boat for himself and camera. You and I will take our guns, Haines, and see if we can't get a shot. What do you say?"

"Capital!" said Haines, and as I echoed the sentiment the motion was declared to be carried.

The sun was beginning to sink in the heavens, and the sultry heat of the day exchanged for a languid, pleasant temperature, before the gig was launched and manned by her swarthy crew. Camera, double backs, a "wide-angle" and "rapid rectilinear," rifles, shot guns, and provisions were handled promiscuously in, and next moment we found ourselves shooting up the sluggish river with the dark hull of the "Syria" looming up behind us.

Give me a morning in Switzerland, a day in Scotland, an evening in Africa, and a night on the shores of the Mediterranean or in a hill station in India. There is a sensuous langour in the balmy air which resembles the after sensation of a Turkish bath more than anything else which I can compare it to. You lie across the thwarts of the boat watching the blue reek of your pipe curling upwards, and lulled by the measured stroke of the oars. I was in this enviable position, and just summoning up energy enough to quote the "Lotus eaters" –

"Our home
Lies far beyond the deep; we will no longer roam" –

when I hear a duet from Haines and the Captain. "Now, Doctor! There's your chance! Look sharp!" I sprang to my feet and saw "my chance" bearing down upon me in the shape of the King of

Duketown's great war canoe. It came sweeping along with its seventy canoe men, a group of warriors in the stern, a fetish man waving a brush in front clearing the evil spirits out of the way, and his gracious majesty in a kind of pagoda in the centre, with a white top hat, pea jacket, and all the other insignia of royalty. I clutch desperately at drop shutter and lens, while "happy and glorious" takes off his hat in answer to a half-derisive cheer from my two companions. I make a last gallant attempt to secure him, but miss him by a hair's breadth as the great canoe goes swishing round a curve under the combined influence of paddles and current.

This is a disappointment, and I "gird up my loins" with a mental vow not to be caught napping again. It is gall and worm-wood to me to think that the chief mate aboard the "Syria" will have the war canoe safe and snug in his plate-carrier before my return, while I have missed it. The chief mate (I may mention in parenthesis) is another harmless insect – *Scarabœus cameriferus* – and there is a keen rivalry between us. This rivalry is increased by the fact that we are working on different systems. I develop as I go in an extemporised dark room, while he, following the lead of Colonel Stuart Wortley and other travellers in the tropics, re-serves his negatives until his return. I have already, I think, mentioned my belief that the latent image always fades to a certain extent, and that a very different result is brought about when plates are developed shortly after exposure to what obtains when they are reserved for some months. That, however, is a matter which can only be settled by a consensus of individual experiences. Chafing over my failures I get the camera ready, while my two companions clear for action and stand to their guns; for we are paddling along the edge of the forest, and there is every prospect of game.

None of us are disappointed. I lead of by a characteristic "bit," which would serve as an epitome of the whole western coast – a dark lane of water, with the gloomy mangrove trees meeting overhead, and the slow, turbid current eddying about their roots, while every vile creature born of vegetable putrescence crawls upon the slimy bank. Dante might have made another circle in hell to rival the frozen stream and the burning marl, had he ever realised the horrors of an African swamp. I am mildly chaffing my companions on having drawn first blood, when their artillery opens with a roar, and a couple of gorgeous kingfishers, light blue and green, come fluttering down into the river. We pass a native woman drifting down in her canoe, with a basket of palm nuts for the traders at Old Calabar. I put up the rapid lens and shutter, focus for "distance," and resume the lead by transferring the swarthy dame to the tell-tale plate; but the Captain equalises matters by the death of a magnificent squirrel, and the purser knocks over a bird resembling a snipe with a very long shot, which became longer every subsequent occasion on which he narrated the anecdote.

We are passing some thick and tangled brushwood now, when there is a sudden alarm among our negro crew, and the steersman gives a sweep with his paddle which takes us half-a-dozen yards from the bank.

"What is it, eh?" "A snake massa! There him be – there, on dem bush!" There he was, sure enough – an enormously-exaggerated worm livid in colour, with a couple of little beady eyes and a tongue that flickered venomously in front of him. Up go the two shot-guns.

"Stop a minute, do!" I implored, as I wrestled frantically with the camera; but there is no restraining the ardour of the sportsmen, and before I can change the lens and focus him the reptile is floating down the stream with his back broken, and my photographic novelty is lost for ever.

Another couple of miles are passed without yielding anything of importance. Now and again we see the long eddy of an alligator, or his sharp snout appears for a moment above the thick water, but the monarch of the mud is too wary for either rifle or camera. We pull through a series of lagoons, and then, as we come round a bend of the river, we see a great native village in front of us. The captain tells us that it is called Creektown, and that on the occasion of his last visit to it he saw a poor wretch buried in an ant-heap by order of the king, from which his skeleton was dug out in a few hours picked perfectly clean. We land with a resolution – on my part, at least – to have as little as possible to say to his majesty.

It is curious to see the effect which a photograph has upon the perfectly-untutored mind. I have frequently observed it on the coast when showing natives prints of places with which they were familiar from their infancy. A portrait would be hailed with roars of delight; but landscape was a dead letter among them, and I have never known a savage recognise a place from its representation. Appreciation of perspective seems to be entirely a matter of training and cultivation. The savage eye sees a large hut and a small one in the picture before it, but the undeveloped brain fails to draw the inference that the small one is small because it is further away. Children and artists in the early days of art always depicted every object as being on the same plane. I have frequently observed in Africa that the first thing a native does when you show him a landscape is to turn it round and look at the other side of it. What the exact object of this manœuvre may be I do not pretend to know, but the action is so unvarying and universal – whether among Kroomen, Mandingoes, Houssars, Ashantees, or any other tribe – that there must be the same good reason for it. Oliver Wendell Holmes formulated the proposition that every equal brain with similar factors to work on will evolve the same product, and the remark seems to hold good among the wild tribes of the coast.

With the exception of the natives, who have been demoralised by contact with the traders and by the brutality of the slave trade, the inhabitants of the dark continent are really a quiet and in-offensive race of men, whose whole ambition is to be allowed to lead an agricultural life, unmolested and in peace. That, at least, is the opinion which I have formed of them, not only from what I have seen but from frequent conversation with the more intel-ligent chiefs who had travelled in the interior. My firm belief is that an unarmed, unescorted Englishman could travel without let or hindrance through the length and breadth of Africa. Kings, have, however, a very natural objection to large parties, armed to the teeth with formidable weapons, forcing their way through their dominions. This is why they begin to get their stew-pans and sauce-bottles ready when they see a Stanley or any other modern explorer coming down on them.

On landing at the village, one of the first objects that met our view was a very ancient and supernaturally-ugly hag, who was lying under a sort of cow-shed with heavy iron manacles round her wrists and ankles and a chain connecting them, which might have been a piece of the cable of the "Syria." What this unfor-tunate woman had done we were unable to find out, but the punishment was being inflicted by order of the king. I need hardly say that I lost no time in adding her to my collection – a proceeding which she seemed most strenuously to object to. Her captivity she was reconciled to, but that a real, live, white man should come and put up a three-legged fetish in front of her was more than she could bear. In spite of kind words and many coppers we could hear her howls – "linked sweetness long drawn out" – for some time after she had disappeared from view.

We were rather amused to find that the king had erected a large building dedicated to the Devil, in close proximity to the church. He was nominally a Christian, but used to go on alternate Sundays to the two different establishments. The idea of "hedg-ing" in matters of religion had evidently never occurred to his imperial mind. If he went to heaven, well and good; but if he were unfortunate enough to be consigned to the other place, at least the Devil could not have the heart to do him much damage after he had built him a house.

My view of Creektown, which included both of these rival edifices was unfortunately rather spoiled by the chalky effect produced by the missionary's house and one or two other white-washed buildings. I was the more disappointed because I had generally found the soft light of the setting sun most adapted for photography in Africa, and especially useful in toning down crude, hard colours and staring outlines. The failure in giving idea of distance so common in tropical countries is also rectified to a certain extent by working in the evening, and is minimised by the introduction of the gelatine process. The resident missionary, whom we proceeded to visit, proved to be a capital fellow and seemed delighted at our appearance, a new white face being a rare sight in his parish.

The light was waning now and no more negatives were to be had, so that I was able to settle myself down to a quiet pipe without any *arrière pensèe*. Our entertainer told us much that was interesting about life in the interior and his journeyings there. One of his anecdotes struck me as being amusing. The Captain had been anxiously inquiring about heavy game, to which the missionary answered that he had only once seen an elephant on the banks of the river, and never wished to see another. "I'm not much of a shot," he said, apologetically. "You see, the beast was standing among some bushes, so I went ashore with the heavy rifle and got as near him as I could. There were some flies bothering him, so he kept moving about, wagging his little stump of a tail. At last he stood still, with his head in the air and his tail standing straight up, so I 'let fly.' The bullet must have passed over its head, for it hit the tail and snapped it clean off like a carrot. If I had aimed at it, it would have been a magnificent shot. The animal was too aston-ished to be vindictive, and when last I saw him he was leaning against a tree, apparently trying to recall the circumstances which led up to this painful affair. I made for the boat as fast as I could scamper, and very glad I was to find myself safe and sound inside it."

It was almost night time before we took our leave of the hospit-able clergyman and made our way down to the boat. We passed the house of the Devil and the still disconsolate prisoner, and were hailed by a cheer from our crew, who, during our absence, had drunk decidedly more rum than was good for them. We pushed off into the stream, and were just starting on our return when we made out a tall warrior gesticulating on the bank. He had come down to inform us that the king was waiting to see us.

"Confound the king!" remarked the Captain.

"Supper's waiting on board," said Haines.

I am not proud. I thought of the man in the ant-hill and threw in my vote for avoiding his majesty, and the measure was carried. We explained to the ambassador that if the king waited until he saw us he would have one of the finest opportunities of waiting that might ever occur to him. With that, and a strong conviction that "Britons never, never, never," &c., we swung the boat round and went gliding rapidly down the broad, glistening stream, till a few scattered lights and a dark hull rising out of the water in front of us informed us that Old Calabar and the "Syria" were reached once more.

There was a scrambling up the latter, a delicate handing of plate-carriers, and a few anxious inquiries from my fellow amateur, who chuckled much on learning that the war canoe had escaped me. And so to supper, with the satisfied feeling produced by half-a-dozen negatives in the background (most of which, I may mention, gave very excellent results), and the consciousness of an evening both pleasantly and usefully spent.

DRY PLATES ON A WET MOOR

———— ❖ ————

My esteemed friend, whom I shall call the "Commodore," as he is known to a small circle under that *soubriquet*, is a man who is always toiling painfully along some twenty years in the rear of the main body of the human family. I am sure he will not take umbrage at my remark, but rather be the first to acknowledge its truth. Railways and telegraphs have gradually begun to overcome the *vis inertiæ* of the Commodore's mind and to obtrude themselves as undeniable facts, but that is apparently the last concession which he will allow to progress, and he fiercely resents any allusion to telephones, electric lights, and other departures from the ways of our ancestors. He has the courage of his convictions, too, as is to be seen by the shares in which he eagerly invests, having at last made up his mind that, as a lighting power, coal gas is preferable to oil. This being the character of the man, it is not surprising that as a photographer he is an ardent supporter of collodion, and revels in every process which the rest of the fraternity have agreed to abandon. There is something majestic in his conservative scorn for improvement, and he looks upon a gelatine-bromide plate very much as a chevalier of the old *régime* might have gazed upon a *bonnet rouge* of the republic. Still, those who have seen the Commodore's results will allow that he has something to justify him in his opinions, and that skilful manipulation is independent of any process.

When the Commodore strode into my apartment in the middle of August, and interrupted me in retouching a batch of plates, I knew that something was up. He is not a demonstrative man; on the contrary, his emotions are all deeply seated and seldom show upon the surface, but it was evident that he was in high spirits and bursting with some piece of information. I mischievously left him to simmer for some time upon a chair, while I finished my retouching.

"Well, Commodore," I said at last, "what is it?"

The murder was soon out. The office were to have a holiday after their ten months' servitude at the desk – only for three days, it is true but still a holiday. The Commodore had been brushing up his fossil apparatus, and was bent upon a short campaign among the wilds. He had come up to know if I would accompany him. Dartmoor was to be the destination, and the train started within an hour and a half.

"Awfully short notice," he said, apologetically, "but we weren't sure about it ourselves until this afternoon, and then I had to get my things together and put on my travelling togs." The Commodore here waved his hand complacently to indicate the togs in question, the principal articles of which consisted of a broad-brimmed lawn-tennis hat and a pair of corduroy knickerbockers – a combination which suggested a cross between Oscar Wilde and a gamekeeper, though the simple-minded wearer evidently regarded it as pregnant with danger to the susceptibilities of the opposite gender.

"He who hesitates is lost." I made a rush for my apparatus, and began packing it into the smallest available space – an operation which long practice rendered an easy one. Within a quarter of an hour I was standing in full marching order, ready for every photographic emergency.

And now another difficulty arose. The Commodore is not a conversationalist. Though more lively than the proverbial tomb-stone, he is taciturn when compared with an eight-day clock. Clearly a third companion was a necessity. I explained my views upon the subject, and they met with a ready recognition. We both agreed that the "Genius" was the very man who would meet all the requirements of the case.

After locking up my rooms, and bidding an affecting farewell to my landlady, who was too much overcome to make any remark beyond a request for five shillings for the milkman, we sallied forth upon our expedition. The "Genius" – so called on account of some undeveloped opinions supposed to savour of the divine afflatus, and a very much over-developed propensity for con-cocting chemical curiosities with a weird smell and objectionable properties – readily consented to form one of the party. His kit took rather longer to arrange, but, by judicious driving and a reckless disregard for all bye-laws and regulations, we managed to spring into a second-class carriage of the evening train for Plymouth just a second or two before she rolled out of the station.

My list of necessaries was not a cumbersome one. A Meagher's 5 x 4 camera, a Dallymeyer's rapid rectilinear, and three double dark slides were the more important items. My plates I had prepared myself by the boiling method of Mr. W.B. Bolton, and these, with two ferrotype dishes, half-a-pound of hypo., and a couple of two-ounce bottles – the one containing glycerine and pyrogallic acid, and the other ammonia and bromide – completed my equipment. The Genius was found, upon comparison, to be furnished in a very similar manner, save that his lens was a Ross's rapid symmetrical, and his plates Edwards's XLs. I shall refrain from describing the preparations of the conservative Commodore. The camera might have helped Noah to wile away his forty monotonous days had the patriarch been of a scientific turn and the light a little more favourable, while the remainder of his belongings impressed the mind with an awesome feeling of the strides of civilisation and the comparative barbarity of our ancestors.

The Genius is as good a little fellow as ever breathed, but there is no standing his scientific speculations. Three is an awkward number in a railway carriage, as only two can stretch themselves upon the seats, and the third is pinned up uncomfortably in a corner. Our little friend found himself in this position, and, after eyeing us malevolently as we settled our rugs under our heads, he cleared his throat in a menacing manner, and proceeded to detail to us his reason for refusing to believe that chlorine was an element. He paused, however, on remarking the ghastly expression which had come over the Commodore's countenance, and then complained that some one had given him a severe kick in the ribs – an idea which haunted him for the remainder of the journey, and which no amount of argument was sufficient to dispel from his mind.

In the first grey light of morning we found ourselves in the great Devonshire seaport, and were conveyed with our "belongings" to the Royal Hotel, where we turned in just as the other inmates were thinking of rising. A few hours' sleep proved a wonderful restorative, and when after a hearty breakfast, we sallied out to show ourselves upon the Hoe, we were hardly recognisable as the tired travellers of the morning. The Commodore stalked proudly along in that heart-breaking hat and the knickerbockers suggestive of blighted affections, while the Genius trotted by his side, pulling frantically at his incipient moustache, as if under the impression that it might be elongated by pure muscular exertion. I was the only one true to the objects of our journey, and lugged my camera along with me, to the undisguised disgust of my companions.

I was amply rewarded, however, for my disregard of public

opinion. The lovely scene may still be imprinted upon the recollection of my companions – the deep blue of the harbour, the wooded slopes of Mount Edgecumbe, the rough outline of Drake's Island, and away beyond the breakwater the great stretch of ocean reaching to the horizon, where two dark pinnacles indicated the position of the Eddystone light. But the retina is a poor and fleeting receiver of impressions, while the scene which I carried off in my carrier will be before me for many a year to come.

But another and more expected photographic treat was in store for me. As we sauntered down in the direction of the dockyard we came across an excited crowd eagerly "craning" their necks along the water's edge. Every fort and bastion and possible coigne of vantage was lined by spectators, and the crews of the "Cambridge" and other old-fashioned line-of-battle ships clustered upon the yards. Before we could inquire the reason of this excitement a great prow came looming round the corner of the winding channel, and a glorious troopship, radiant in white and blue and gold, steamed slowly down the stream, with a knot of willing little tugs crowding and pushing in front of her, the tops of their funnels hardly level with the deck of their gigantic charge. The "red-coats" clustered like bees upon the shrouds and their cheers were echoed back from the men of war and the crowds upon the shore. My humble little tribute to the general uproar consisted in the click of a spring shutter, and I glanced round triumphantly at my companions as one who is conscious of having reaped the reward of his virtue. Alas! in matters photographic man proposes, but there are several agents which do the other thing. In this case the agent consisted of a too-officious guardian of the peace, who at the critical moment had passed his hand over a portion of the field in a menacing gesture to some mischievous urchin. In spite of the fogging produced I was able ultimately to recover enough to serve at least as some slight reminiscence of the campaign of 1882.

I should like to have spent the whole day in the old historical sea town, taking its curiosities and those numberless "bits" in which it is richer than any town in the south of England. It was strange to see the very alehouses still standing upon the Barbican, in which the bearded and bejewelled filibusters of Drake and Hawkins had squandered the doubloons which they risked their lives for upon the Spanish Main. The Commodore, however, had no appreciation of the romance of history, and the Genius made dark innuendoes as to my real motives in lingering lovingly about the old "pubs.;" so, finding myself in a minority, I was compelled to withdraw my motion for prolonging our stay. We had luncheon at the hotel, and then, having strapped our *impedimenta* upon our shoulders, we struck out into the country with the air of men who were attempting to beat the six days' pedestrian record.

The pace was killing while it lasted, but, unfortunately, it only lasted for a mile and a-half, at the end of which time we all sat down simultaneously upon the slope of one of the outlying forts. My companions stared gloomily back at the city behind us; but a return would be too ignominious, so we proceeded to justify our halt by taking the view. It was a glorious seascape, with just a few bunches of gorse and heather upon the shoulder of the hill to serve as a foreground, while the coast line from the Eddystone to the Start lay like a map before us, framing in the broad stretch of ocean, dotted with sails. None of our results did justice to the exquisite original, though all were fairly good in their way. I see mine hanging upon the wall before me as I write. Clear enough it is, and accurate in detail; but, oh! the dismal greys and whites! Are we never to have the yellow of the sand and the green of the grass and the blue of the ocean transferred to our plates? It seems to me that a standing fund should be put by as a reward, to attract the researches of chemists and physicists in that direction, just as one awaits the fortunate discoverer of the Pole.

Stifling the unworthy temptation to return to our luxurious hotel, we strode sturdily northwards in the direction of the Moor. As we advanced the character of the scenery began to change. Rugged "tors" and tangled masses of half-withered vegetation shut us in, and the narrow road wound through a wilderness in which the only living creatures seem to be a few half-starved Devonshire sheep, who eyed us curiously, as if speculating upon our motives for intruding upon their domains. Wild and stern as was the scene there was a certain rough beauty in it all, and several charming little nooks and corners were secured by our ever-watchful cameras. The enormous number of white sign posts fixed at the angle where every sheep-path departed from the main track told a grim story of the byegone dangers of the Moor – where men had wandered in circles until they had dropped dead of hunger and fatigue. Indeed, with all these precautions, during the last twelve months there have been at least three cases of individuals having met with a similar fate.

The long summer evening was drawing to a close before we trudged into the pretty little village of Roborough, where we had determined to put up for the night. The old English inn – with its signpost of Admiral Vernon and a kitchen door left artfully open to waft a savoury odour into the street – was so irresistible that it was fortunate we had pre-arranged to make it our head-quarters. There with cameras stacked in the corner, and discarded plate-carriers and knapsacks, we indulged in all the luxury of a lounge and well-earned smoke while a substantial tea-dinner was in process of preparation. There was something in the old-world flavour of the whole place which was so congenial to the tastes of the conservative Commodore that I quite expected to hear him propose that our expedition should terminate there and then, and the remainder of the holiday be spent in this luxurious little wayside tavern. However, he rose superior to the temptation, and sketched out our programme for the morrow with the air of a man suffering for conscience sake.

In an ivy-clad, little red-brick cottage, close to the inn, dwells an eccentric villager who dabbles in photography, and ekes out his scanty income by executing villainous prints of rustic beauties and their beaux. We called upon him after our meal, and struck up an intimacy with him on the strength of our common pursuit. He was a grave, white-haired, nature's gentleman, and did the honours of his primitive dark room with an old-fashioned courtesy which delighted the Commodore and myself, the Genius having suddenly vanished – possibly with the ulterior object of making the closer acquaintance of one of those same belles upon whom our venerable entertainer was wont to practice. Even the Commodore seemed progressive to this old rustic enthusiast, who still adhered to every rule and process which existed when the art was in its infancy. Swan's "thirty-time" plates and Dallmeyer's cameras and lenses were a sealed book to him, and he met all my attempts at explanation with a smile of ineffable complacency blended with amusement, as if to intimate that he was too old a bird to be caught by such chaff. As the Commodore rather aided and abetted him in his heresies, I am afraid that the patriarch did not derive much benefit from my lecture upon the relative value of the processes.

There are disadvantages even in old-fashioned inns and antiquated four-post beds, as we found to our cost during the watches of the night. As the Genius expressed it – "We felt a bit 'crowded' at first, but there was more room when we had given the sheets a shaking." However, the healthy exercise which we had taken triumphed eventually over every obstacle, and we strode forth in the morning like giants refreshed, bearing away in our knapsacks a goodly bottle of milk and a plentiful store of bread for our luncheon on the Moor.

Leaving Roborough behind us, we pushed steadily northward through a waste even more delicate than that which we traversed the day before. For ten miles neither house nor inhabitant met our eyes – nothing but a long, undulating plain covered with scanty vegetation; and intersected by innumerable peaty brooks, which meandered down to help to form the Plymouth "leat," constructed by the great Sir Francis Drake, and still used as the only means of water supply. The scene, monotonous as it was, had an interest in my eye as being the seat of several of the incidents in Kingsley's *Westward Ho!* It was along one of these winding, uncertain tracts that Amyas Leigh rode across with his shipmates from Plymouth to Bideford, and the spot where Salvation Yeo slew the King of the Gubbins must have lain a very little to the northward. Now and again, as we reached the summit of some eminence, we had a magnificent view of the country we had passed through, stretching away down to the sea, while on the left the silver Tamar curled along between its thickly-wooded banks. The weather was perfect from a photographic point of view, with just brightness enough to answer every purpose without running a danger of a chalky effect from the whitewashed farm-houses in the distance. We each expended more than one plate upon the glorious landscape, but my very best negative was afterwards ruined by air-bubbles in the developer. Owing to the poverty of the light and a red bull's-eye lantern (and a very poor one at that), I was unable to notice these until they had pitted the plate in a way which was far more suggestive of eruptive fevers than of the glories of nature. Since then I have never used the glycerine pyro developer, as the viscosity produced by the glycerine seems to me to be the sole cause of this defect. I have also learned partially to restrain that photographic impetuosity which prompts me to develop without waiting for the conveniences of my own little workshop.

Had we been told that those were to be the last efforts of our trip we should have laughed the idea to scorn; but alas! a change came over the spirit of our dream. A dusky cloud, which had lain low and threatening along the whole eastern horizon, began gradually to throw out long, ragged tentacles in our direction, which coalesced until they covered the whole heaven, and then with a swish down came a mighty torrent of rain, which soaked us through before we had time to remove our knapsacks and take shelter in our mackintoshes. It had evidently set in wet, so, with heads bowed to the blast and collars buttoned about our necks we staggered along in the direction in which we knew that Tavistock lay. I don't think any of us are ever likely to forget that eight-mile trudge. The thought of the "I told you so's" of certain good friends who had seen us off at the station, and had warned us of the vicissitudes of the "wet moor," added gall and wormwood to our sufferings. When we found ourselves at last in the streets of the picturesque town our plates were the only dry things in our possession, and three sorrier figures could not have been picked out in the length and breadth of England. The sight of the Commodore, with the water streaming down his rakish hat, and with the glory departed from the mud-bespattered knicker-bockers, was almost enough to console the Genius and myself for all our misfortunes.

However, "all's well that ends well." A good dinner and a stiff glass of whisky and water – whisky without the water was suggested by the Genius, as our systems were already permeated by the milder liquid – soon set us on our legs again, and we retired to rest with great resolutions for the morrow. One glance at the streaming window panes in the morning dissipated every hope of being able to finish our third day. The rain was still pouring down in the way we knew so well. With heavy hearts we were forced to acknowledge that the game was up, and a hermetically-sealed four-wheeler bore us off with our effects to catch the midday train for home.

There was nothing remarkable in a photographic sense in this little tour. As I have already mentioned, several of the plates from which I had expected most met with mishaps and disappointed me. I think, however, that this sketch of the doings of the Commodore, the Genius, and myself may, at least, have the effect of showing what an amount of experience and what varied photographic opportunities may be compressed into a very short space of time. Even a three days' holiday may remain a pleasant reminiscence for ever if the time be well utilised. I think, further, that the readers of THE BRITISH JOURNAL OF PHOTOGRAPHY might choose some better hunting ground than the "wet moor" – a concession which, however, none of us would admit to the commiserating friends who welcomed us on our return.

A FEW TECHNICAL HINTS

EMULSIFYING. – I have found no method of emulsification so good as that recommended by Mr. W.K. Burton, but not, I believe, originated by him. This process consists in dropping the nitrate of silver in crystals into the bromide solution and shaking until the crystals are entirely dissolved. The emulsion thus formed will always be found to be ruby red by transmitted light.

BOILING. – The common notion, that the length of time during which emulsion may be boiled with advantage is limited to about thirty minutes, is a complete mistake. If the solutions be made slightly acid, as recommended by the Editor of the ALMANAC, and if there be a small amount of iodide in the emulsion, as advised by Captain Abney, boiling may be continued with advantage for one or even two hours, especially if the emulsion be in a not too concentrated form.

WASHING. – If an emulsion which is in a fine state of division be washed only for a few minutes, but during that time be kept in constant motion, it is more thoroughly purified from the soluble bromide, iodide, and nitrates than could possibly have been accomplished by a long period of soaking without movement or in a coarse state of division. The emulsion, too, is liable to be deteriorated by a prolonged soaking.

COATING THE PLATES. – the plates should be thickly coated – at least so thickly that the form of the dark room lamp flame cannot be distinguished through the film when it is wet. The advantages of a thick film are as well known as they are enormous, if the emulsion be of good quality. If, however, it be defective all defects will be increased by the thickness of the film. Thus, fogs – whether chemical, green, red, yellow, or otherwise – will show in a ratio which is directly proportionate to this thickness.

DRYING. – In drying, the great object aimed at should be to obtain a thoroughly-brisk current of air well distributed among the plates. If this be secured and the drying-box placed in a perfectly dry spot there is no need for artificial heat, even in winter. Plates so dried – that is, with an ample current of air at atmospheric temperature – never frill, unless the gelatine from which they have been made has been absolutely rotten.

FRILLING. – Frilling of the most obstinate character – even such as makes its appearance in the developing solution – may be prevented by mixing the developer with a certain amount of methylated spirit. Rinse the plate afterwards with a small quantity of methylated spirit and water, and place it in a mixture of a saturated solution of chrome alum and methylated spirit. The quantity of methylated spirit in all these solutions may vary from ten to twenty-five per cent., according to the obstinacy of the malady. With the latter quantity development will be greatly protracted.

TRIAL OF BURTON'S EMULSION PROCESS

As the above process, though introduced to the notice of the photographic world by my friend Mr. W.K. Burton as far back as the 14th of November, in an address delivered at the meeting of the Photographic Society of Great Britain, is still to a certain extent *sub judice*, a few remarks upon it by one who has given it a careful and unprejudiced trial may not be out of place. In every branch of science there is a danger that what claims to be an improvement may really be a retrograde movement, and this holds good particularly of photography. I do not think, however, that Burton's emulsion process can by any possibility be placed in this category of equivocal innovations.

Winter is, *par excellence*, the season for manufacture of emulsions. The cold is advantageous, while actual photography being at its minimum the photographer cannot do better than prepare for future campaigns. Though lack of time has caused me to fall back on commercial plates of late, it has been my custom, as far as possible to prepare a stock during the winter months which should suffice for the whole of the summer.

With this laudable object I was about to start with my old favourite, the boiling process, when I noticed the publication of Mr. W.K. Burton's modification. It recommended itself to me at once as being an improvement over everything which had gone before. The only objection which I could see against it was the great length of time from the beginning to the end of the manipulation, and this in my own case proved to be a positive advantage; for, having my time taken up with professional business, and being liable to interruption, I have under any circumstances to extend my operations over several evenings. Observe particularly that, in Mr. Burton's process, although the whole time needed is comparatively long, still that occupied in actual manipulation is shorter than is the case in any ordinary process. It commends itself to a busy man or to any amateur, situated like myself, with intermittent and irregular periods of leisure.

The details of the process have been already dwelt upon in THE BRITISH JOURNAL OF PHOTOGRAPHY, but still I may briefly recapitulate them for the benefit of anyone who may, notwithstanding, be hazy as to the details. Any formula may be retained during the early part of the process, as the special features are only introduced after the boiling is completed. Mr. Burton recommends, however, the employment of an unusually large amount of water, under the impression that it favours a fine state of division in the bromide of silver – a supposition in which I consider him to be perfectly correct. After cooling the emulsion down to 120° Fahr., or thereabouts, strong ammonia and alcohol are added. This causes the bromide of silver to be precipitated, and the solution containing the gelatine and soluble salts may be poured off. This process is repeated, the former precipitate being stirred up in a fresh quantity of water, and allowed to settle once more. It is then washed by decantation, mixed with gelatine, and the emulsion is complete.

An excellent rough-and-ready method of improvising the necessary boiling apparatus is to use a jam pot covered by an inverted flower-pot saucer, and place standing in a good large saucepan with the lid on and half full of water. The whole is placed upon an ordinary cooking burner. This arrangement will be found to answer quite as well as a more pretentious one, and to give most satisfactory results. In this manner I have prepared plates more rapid than any I have got before, and of excellent quality. The emulsion needs some keeping, however, before it attains its maximum of sensitiveness. I find that, as a rule, the plates will not stand so strong a developer as pure, boiled emulsion plates; but, on the other hand, they will give density with a weaker one.

I have read with considerable interest a communication upon *superficial fog* in THE BRITISH JOURNAL OF PHOTOGRAPHY, by the originator of this process. In it he remarks that it only makes its appearance in the case of emulsions which are very rapid, and which are capable of giving dense images with clear shadows. My experience entirely corroborates Mr. Burton's researches in this matter. I have formed my own conclusions, however, as to the cause of the phenomenon. I believe it to be due to alkalinity of the emulsion, combined with the predisposing nature of the silver bromide. It is, I find, by no means uniformly amenable to the treatment recommended, namely, the addition of alcohol and preservative, though this has undoubtedly very frequently the desired effect. I find that the addition of any mineral acid (hydro-chloric, for example) to neutralise the alkalinity of the emulsion, will invariably cure it. Care must be taken in adding it, however, as any considerable excess of acid has the effect of slowing the plates, and should, therefore, be avoided.

Another point worthy of notice in connection with the addition of acid is that ammonia has to be added to the emulsion to cause it to ripen by keeping. Hydrochloric acid is added to neutralise this ammonia, and, of course, chloride of ammonium in the film is the result. This, it must be remembered, is a powerful restrainer, so that the less there is of it present the better for the efficiency of the emulsion. The least possible quantity of ammonia, therefore, should be added in the first instance.

I have read the excellent editorial article, which holds out some prospect of doing away with the ammonia and of requiring a shorter time for precipitation. I shall certainly try it, and shall, with the Editor's permission, give the result to your readers in a future communication.

SOUTHSEA: THREE DAYS IN SEARCH OF EFFECTS

---◆---

Of all seasons of the year commend me to Easter as the time best adapted for a pleasant and instructive little photographic tour. The air is cold enough to brace the sinews and make the pedestrian stride lustily forth without numbing the hand in which he holds his portable leather case. There is a sun above him bright enough to produce a moral effect without scorching his face and moistening his brow. Spring is rising up all round. The birds are singing and the hedgerows blossoming. There are changing effects of light and cloud, sunshine and rain. To wind up, everything is *en fête* and there are studies of life to be secured as interesting as anything in nature. Taking it all in all, the vagrant searcher after the beautiful could hardly choose a better time for his peregrinations.

So thought my two friends, "The Man of Science" and "The Lunatic" (any nearer clue to their identity might be invidious, especially in view of some of their future proceedings). As March dragged its slow length along many a heated discussion was held as to the place to be done and how to do it, in which the rival merits of Brighton, Eastbourne and other watering-places were eagerly discussed. The question might never have been settled had an invitation not arrived from a provincial friend of photographic propensities whom we shall name "The Doctor," in which he proposed that his house at Southsea should be made head-quarters of the party, and that they should choose the banks of the Solent as the scene of their operations. The proposal was too tempting to be refused, and the night train upon Good Friday found our two photographers clutching desperately to their somewhat bulky apparatus, and struggling with a dense crowd of bony-elbowed excursionists who were bound for the same direction. "Not angels, but angles," "The Lunatic" remarked in an outburst of sanity, as he stowed his gear on the rack and rolled his eye upon his fellow-travellers in a homicidal fashion.

Southsea is a geographical expression which it might puzzle a good many people to define. That it is a watering-place within an attainable distance of London is generally known, but its exact size is vaguely appreciated save by those who have had the pleasure of visiting it; and this vagueness is intensified when the inquirer demands his railway ticket and finds that none are issued to any place of the name. As a matter of fact Southsea is an offshoot of Portsmouth, and has not been honoured by an independent station, although in point of size it is second only to Brighton, and when taken in conjunction with Portsmouth very much surpasses it. There is something piquant and interesting in this union between a grim old fortified town, grey with age and full of historical reminiscences, and a brand new fashionable watering-place, resplendent with piers, parades and hotels. Apart from sentiment, it promises a variety to the vagrant photographer which can hardly be matched by any single town of my acquaintance.

Before going further let me run over briefly the "kit" chosen by my visitors, for I may acknowledge my identity with "The Doctor," though I prefer the *soubriquet* as giving this little sketch a less egotistical sound. In "The Man of Science" our little party boasted the presence of one of the leading dry-plate workers of the day, and the holder of the name which is familiar wherever THE BRITISH JOURNAL OF PHOTOGRAPHY circulates – a tolerably wide range. His preparations were naturally more pretentious than those of his companions. He used a Rouch's camera fitted for 12 x 10 plates, though 10 x 8 were used for instantaneous work. The lens was a Ross's rapid symmetrical of sixteen inches focus, provided with an instantaneous shutter of the ordinary drop form, but having the peculiarity that it was so arranged as to drop from three different heights in such a way as to give exposures of varying lengths. The shutter intended to give a comparatively long exposure dropped only a quarter of an inch before opening, so as to have little momentum. The medium exposure was effected by a drop of about two inches. The most rapid had a drop of four inches, the latter giving one-twelfth of a second exposure. During our tour the shortest exposure was always used, the lens being worked sometimes at $^1/_{16}$ – that is sixteen of the uniform standard of the Photographic Society of Great Britain, or occasionally even at thirty-two of the same. In every case the exposures were ample.

"The Lunatic" – whose lunacy, by the way, never manifested itself until late in the evening, when he would dance weird dances and exhibit a desire to shake hands with every able-bodied citizen that he met – was content with a more portable "kit." He used a half-plate camera of Lancaster's make, and also a quarter-plate camera. His lens was a single view, with a diaphragm of $1/32$, or sixty four of the uniform standard. He used rapid hand exposures as far as possible, and these were found in most cases to be rather over- than under-exposed. Curiously enough, though yachts were taken many times during the tour when in rapid motion crossing the field near the camera, they all came out sharp. This shows the absurdity of the idea commonly held that an exposure as short as one-eightieth or one-hundredth part of a second is necessary to get ships in motion. In this case the exposures were probably never shorter than from one-quarter to one-sixth of a second, to attain which requires a skilful manipulation of the lens cap. Among the successes achieved by this member of the party may be mentioned a group in the open air taken with a hand exposure at $\frac{1}{16}$.

Southsea was reached at midnight, where two or three genial and hospitable friends awaited the arrival of the travellers, who insisted upon what "The Man of Science" described as an "extended trial of the wet process," and it was not until fairly on the Common with the next morning's breeze playing merrily across it that some symptoms of vitality began to show themselves in the party.

My own apparatus had little to distinguish it beyond its weather-beaten appearance, arising from the fact of its owner having walked to and fro in the world like a well-known historical character whose intentions were less laudable. I have already had the honour of describing it in the Journal. I may remark, however, that I have recently adopted a changing-box in place of dark slides, and find the arrangement very satisfactory. I do not trouble to cover the whole of my apparatus with a focussing-cloth, but manipulate my camera and changing-box without the smallest fear in bright sunlight. In fact, I may say here that, in my opinion, very unnecessary precautions are taken generally. I find that, though both my friends discarded the use of the focussing-cloth entirely after the mere operation of focussing was performed, and handled their dark slides in the light, none of their negatives were ever fogged except in the cases of evident overexposure.

The morning was a bright and cheerful one, with just enough of cloud piled up in the horizon to make an effective seascape, in which each of the party immediately indulged. The broad Solent, with its three circular forts, its fleets of yachts, and its sullen-looking men-of-war, all backed up by the long slopes of the Isle of Wight, made as pretty a picture as an artist's eye could desire. Our next attempt was on the Ryde steamer, which came ploughing along in the fair-way about a couple of hundred yards from the shore, the decks black with excursionists, and the foam flying from the paddles. Owing to her sudden appearance, "The Lunatic," with his quick hands and small camera, was the only one who succeeded in securing her satisfactorily. Wandering along the beach we had hoped to catch a few effects from yachts in motion; but we were temporarily disappointed as the rising wind prevented most of them from leaving their anchorage. In spite of this drawback our morning was by no means a barren one, as a brave array of plates would testify. A group of tricyclists, a knot of Highlanders ("South Sea Islanders," as "The Lunatic" facetiously remarked), and several groups of friends lent a variety to a succession of views of the Solent and Spithead. The spectacle of "The Man of Science" endeavouring to take a fractious infant – possibly with the view of conciliating and including its fair holder – was enough to reconcile us to any disappointment, more especially when his attempt to look fascinating threw the unfortunate child into a rigid and cataleptic state, from which it emerged blue but still screaming. By the way, while alluding to the wind I must give a word of praise to the exceedingly light and handy alpenstock stand of Mr. George Smith, which was used by "The Man of Science." It is so marvellously light that no one can credit its steadiness under a 12 x 10 camera, even when a heavy wind was blowing, unless they have tested it. We were all impressed by it as a marvel of handiness and strength.

As the elements were still unfavourable in the afternoon we confined ourselves to indoor work and to developing the plates of the morning, the results of which were for the most part extremely satisfactory. I may mention here that all the pictures were made by Burton's precipitation process, in which I believe more than ever. In the case of my companions, "The Man of Science" had made the emulsion, and each coated his own plates. They were extraordinarily rapid – considerably more so than mine.

After conciliating "The Doctor's" housekeeper by expending a couple of plates on the perpetuation of her charms, and another in taking a charming little group of Blenheim spaniels, an expedition was made to the house of a genial Southsea solicitor, outdoor work being still precluded by the state of the weather. Here a few more groups were taken, and a small musical party was instituted by our hospitable entertainer, which lent variety to the proceedings.

After a Sunday spent quietly, all hands were ready and eager for work on Monday morning. The weather was beautifully fine, with hardly a cloud on the sky, and just breeze enough to be pleasant. Snatching a hurried breakfast we made our way down to the beach, which was black with holiday makers, and where there were many interesting studies to be secured were it not for the nobler game we had in view. "The Doctor" could not resist the temptation of taking one unfortunate individual, who had bound himself securely with a rope and was piteously appealing to the surrounding crowd for a "little encouragement," on receipt of which it was understood that he would emerge from his bonds. His appeal seemed to be feebly responded to by an apathetic public, though, as "The Lunatic" remarked, a handsome sum would have been promptly raised for the purpose of keeping him in confinement for the remainder of his natural existence. Our original intention had been to keep to the beach and take our chance of yachts standing in near enough to make a good picture. Through the good offices of our legal friend, however, we obtained an introduction to Mr. Newnham, the principal letter of sailing boats, who showed us the greatest courtesy and attention. This gentleman actually ordered several of his yachts to man-œuvre off the end of a small jetty upon which our cameras were placed, and, although there was a great demand for them at the time, employed them for more than an hour in cruising about in obedience to our requests. Under these circumstances it was little wonder that we obtained some interesting plates, and that the object of our expedition was amply fulfilled.

Our method of taking these yachts in motion was by focussing for the distance, moving the camera to follow the motion of the yacht, and "firing away" at the moment judged to be the right one – not an easy thing to calculate, as I can testify from numerous failures. This procedure is only possible in the case of the comparatively short focus lens. In the case of the long-focus (sixteen inches) one it is not possible to focus for the distance, as, if such were done, the yacht enough to fill any large portion of the plate would be completely out of focus. An element of guess work is thus introduced.

It is wonderful how possible it is in the nervousness of the moment, when you imagine the camera to be so adjusted that the yacht will occupy the centre of the plate, to miss the object completely. Never shall I forget the rage and dismay which disfigured the intellectual face of our "Man of Science" when he scanned the detail coming up on his pet plate, intended to represent the meeting of two clippers going swiftly upon opposite tracks. As he gazed blankly at the single line of horizon which appeared on the picture, unbroken by the semblance of a sail, he rippled forth a series of theological terms – or, rather, in consideration of his profession, we will charitably suppose them to be engineering ones. His was not an isolated case, however, for there was not one of us but had some similar mishap. Only those who have experienced it can realise how easily the accident may occur.

Through Mr. Newnham's kindness we expounded a dozen or more plates, each to excellent advantage, and, having wound up by taking the proprietor himself and a group of all the big leather boots with men in them who congregate about boat-houses, we felt that our morning's work had been a successful one. After luncheon we made the nearer acquaintance of one of Mr. Newnham's craft, and, throwing photography and all that appertains thereto to the dogs, indulged in a glorious sail down the Solent. With a fine press of canvas and a breeze which heeled the little yacht over until her gunwale was almost flush with the water, nothing could be imagined better calculated to clear the lungs of a couple of carbonised Londoners. The only bitter drop in our cup of happiness was the presence of a cynical and saturnine boatman, who insisted upon demonstrating the exact amount of wind which would capsize the boat, which, according to his calculations was just the least puff more than we had at present. Having made this clear to us he stood by with a gloomy yet triumphant expression upon his countenance, and invented lies about the distance which he could swim in case of emergency. Beyond the croaking of this "old man of the sea," however, our trip was a most enjoyable one. Running down to Spithead we cruised round the three forts erected by Lord Palmerston – two of which are iron-clad, and have fresh coatings of metal added on to meet every increase of armour upon any foreign man-of-war. These forts command the only channel by which Portsmouth can be approached, and, being supported by others on the shore, render the place impregnable upon the sea side. Passing the forts we ran out as far as the light-ship, where the isolated keepers seemed delighted to see us and threw us out their letters, ingeniously sandwiched in between biscuits so as to convert them into convenient missiles. Night was falling, and a purple haze lying over the Isle of Wight, in gorgeous contrast with the deep scarlet bands left by the setting sun, before we found ourselves once more upon Southsea beach. There, bidding adieu to the melancholy mariner, we made our way back to headquarters in a ravenous condition, which considerably astonished "The Doctor's" house-keeper.

As our evening was largely spent in developing I may make a few remarks upon that topic in connection with instantaneous work. The subject usually adopted for this is commonly one from which it is somewhat difficult to get a negative giving sufficient contrast. It is true that the highest lights (in our case, for instance, the sails of the yachts) reflect much light; but, on the other hand, even those parts which are to be represented by transparent or almost transparent glass in the negative reflect much also. There is, therefore, no very great range between the highest lights and what takes the place of shadows. It is necessary to compensate for this fact by a suitable developer. One well adapted for the subject of our plates consisted of two or three grains of pyro., one and a-half grains of bromide, and three minims of strong ammonia to the ounce.

While I am on this subject I should like to say a few words on the advisability of using the alum bath, even when the plates have no tendency to frilling. A little hydrochloric acid should be mixed, but not so much as should be used for negatives that have been fixed, as the clearing and decolourising action of the acid appears to be much more powerful on plates that are unfixed than on fixed ones. It is necessary to thoroughly wash the plates after going through the alum bath, or a white powder (presumably sulphur) is deposited by the hypo.

Little work could be done upon the Tuesday, as the London contingent desired to get home by the afternoon, and most of their effects were already packed. A last stroll was taken about the town, however, under the guidance of Mr. Barnden, the well-known superintendent of the Gresham Insurance Society. This gentleman's kind attention and the assiduity with which he held sheets, carried cameras, and infused good humour into everyone was one of the most agreeable incidents of our tour. Several plates were taken in this final expedition, in connection with one of which a curious photographic incident occurred. A small group had been arranged upon the seashore which "The Lunatic" was about to take, when a bright idea seized upon "The Man of Science," and, removing his camera to some little distance, he proceeded to take both photographer and group. "The Doctor," not to be outdone, retired forty or fifty yards, and succeeded in obtaining a picture which included both his companions. The effect was, as may be imagined, somewhat quaint and original.

All things must have an end, and the best of friends must part. The midday train bore away "The Lunatic" and "The Man of Science," with all their goods and chattels, including from forty to fifty excellent plates. From first to last the little trip had been a success, and, imperfect as this account of it is, I trust I have said enough to show that our only difficulty was an *embarras des richesses*. Could we have extended it over a week we should still have found much of photographic interest. I think that the last words of my friends were heartily meant when they assured me that their very next holiday would find them in Southsea once again. I trust that on that occasion we may make up for the deficiencies of this one, and that I may have an opportunity of communicating our results to THE BRITISH JOURNAL OF PHOTOGRAPHY.

TO THE WATERFORD COAST AND ALONG IT

It is only two years ago since I was sitting in my lodgings in the old metropolitan city of Scotland, consuming much tobacco and keeping a contemplative eye upon my last batch of plates which were "cooking" in the setting sun. From my lofty "flat" I commanded a view of a great wilderness of grey roofs topped with red chimneys, every one of them reeking up its contribution of carbon to vitiate my atmosphere. Away across this dreary waste rose the square massive tower of St. Giles, with its gothic top – an admirable object of practice for an embryonic photographer. Had I had a pupil St. Giles might have been to me what Salisbury Cathedral was to Mr. Pecksniff, who caused the budding architects, who had paid him their premiums, to draw it from the Nor'-Nor'-East and the Sou'-Sou'-West, and every other point in the compass from one year's end to another.

I was smiling languidly at the idea when a quick step on the stair and a knock at the door announced my irrepressible friend Cunningham – most enthusiastic of dry-plate workers. There was a look of consequence in his eye as he rolled it round in search of alcoholic refreshment, which denoted some weighty resolve taken or proposition of importance to be evolved.

"Guess where I am going?" he began.

"Gib it up!" I rejoined, with a mild attempt at facetiousness.

"Smith is going and so is Ramsay, and they want you to come too. We are all going to take our cameras and three or four dozen plates and make a regular trip of it."

"Where to?" I asked.

"We reckon we can do the whole thing within a week."

"Where?" I demanded.

"And the best of it is that the whole trip won't run us in for more than about twenty-five shillings travelling expenses right through and back."

"Where to?" I yelled.

"To Ireland, of course," said Cunningham in an aggrieved voice; "I told you that when I came in. Waterford is the place we were thinking of going to."

At first the idea seemed rather an out-of-the-way one; but as I came to talk it over with my friend he advanced a good many arguments in favour of it. A mutual chum of ours named Smith possessed a cousin at Youghal, which cousin possessed a yacht (a "yawl," Cunningham said, but he was always an incorrigible punster). We might reckon on the use of this vessel in coasting along the Waterford shore and from its deck we might do justice to the splendid cliff scenery which characterises both this country and Wexford.

A single ticket from Edinburgh right through to Glasgow, and thence by boat to Waterford, touching at Dublin, came to something well under a pound. I may add that starting from the other end of the chain the boats run from London, *via* Portsmouth, Southampton, and Plymouth, to Waterford, and so on to Glasgow, and I have no doubt that the fare from London to Waterford would be even less than that quoted. For some time I had been intending to give myself a holiday, and when would I get better opportunity? I silently drained Cunningham's glass to the bottom, and held out my hand as a pledge that I would not desert him.

There was little trouble about our "kits." With my old camera and five dozen trustworthy plates, with enough pyro., &c., to do a little test developing, should I wish, I was fully equipped for the campaign. I had a light tripod stand with ball-and-socket joint for outdoor work on land, and an ordinary tripod for all other exigencies. Some of my companions were more ambitious in their preparations, but still the total amount of luggage was not a very formidable one.

We took our through tickets at Cook's tourist office, by which a further saving was effected. The mild-eyed clerk who dispenses them looked at us curiously and remarked that he had not sold many that year, for they were dangerous times in Ireland, and there was little inducement for the Saxon tourist unless he hankered for the absorbing but brief excitement of having his head battered in or otherwise tampered with by the "down-trodden Clan-na-Gael." Every day brought a grim list across the sea of midnight visits, maimed cattle, half-murdered bailiffs, and ruined landlords. These things, however, rather served to inflame our fanatical photographic propensities than to allay them. We saw a glorious vista of character portraits and other novelties stretching out before us. The "foinest pisant in the worrld," or rather an assorted set of samples of that individual – a rack-rent landlord in a state of bloated impecuniosity ("lack-rent" would be a better name for the class) – an agent, or as much of one as the aborigines had left together by the time of our arrival – these and all the other curiosities of Irish life should adorn our collections. Then in still life there would be the ruined homestead, the care-taker's hut, and other signs of the times. It seemed to us, as we stepped gaily into the train at the Caledonian Station and deposited our traps under the seats, that apart from the scenery our trip could hardly fail to have interesting results.

Of the four of us three were photographically inclined. My friend, Ramsay, was the only one who did not dabble in the black art – as an old friend of mine used to call it in the pre-gelatine, hand-staining days. Ramsay, however, was artistically inclined, and carried with him his cardboard and his paints, so that he was safe against *ennui*. Besides, he hunted and fished, and knew enough of photography to appreciate our objects and take an intelligent interest. Though he had no scientific necessities to provide for he indulged in more luggage than all the rest of the party. "He is a fellow of infinite chest," remarked Cunningham ruefully as he surveyed the pile upon the Edinburgh platform.

The run to Glasgow occupied a little more than an hour, and when we arrived there we found that owing to the tide we should not leave by boat for several hours. We had dinner comfortably at a hotel, therefore; and having fallen in with one or two old friends we all proceeded to Greenock together by rail, to await the steamer there. We filled in the interval very pleasantly by wander-ing over the old town and inspecting one of the shipbuilding yards, which we had hardly left before our steamer came churn-ing down the river, and we found ourselves with our chattels on board of the good ship "Rathlin." There was a shouting, a throwing off of warps, and a cheer from our friends on the shore, and we were fairly started for the land of Ire.

I know no such place where a photographer may have such an *embarras des richesses* as on the Clyde in a steamer when the sea is calm. There were hardly any passengers besides ourselves and a few commercial travellers with a couple of young ladies, so that we could plant our cameras where we liked upon the poop. As we steamed along a great moving panorama seemed to be unrolled before us. The huge half-finished ships which lined the bank, with their gaunt ribs sticking up to heaven like skeletons of some antedeluvian saurian, gradually gave place to green meadows and country scenery, which alternated with the pretty little watering places which dot the coast from Greenock to Ardrossan. Steamers from Ireland and America ploughed past us, and a host of little yachts played all round. We wasted several plates in endeavouring to secure some of these as they passed. Even when the camera is on the shore it is surprising how easy it is to miss a large object which is crossing the field. Many a time have I borne home what I imagined to be a splendid plate of yacht or steamer, only to find, as I watched the detail coming up, nothing but a single monotonous line of horizon. When, however, the stand of your camera is also moving at eight or ten miles an hour the difficulty is proportionately increased, and the chances are, as we found, very much against a successful result. Our landscapes, however, and views of the banks were all that could be desired.

As the sun sank down towards the horizon we had got well out to the mouth of the Clyde. The water was as calm as a mill pond and reflected the scarlet tinge of the clouds. Away to the north were the rugged mountains of Argyleshire and of the great islands, wrapped in that purple evening mist which Waller Paton loves. Ahead of us was Arran, whose beauties my friend Dr. Thompson has already recounted in this Journal, with its great peak of Goat Fell enveloped in fleecy clouds. To the south the strange precipitous upheaval called Ailsa Crag reared itself out of the ocean – a grim looking place, which has been the last spot upon earth that the eyes of many a drowning man have rested on. The whole scene was as beautiful a one as an artist could love to dwell upon. Ramsay produced his paint-box, and certainly put our whites and greys to shame for the nonce with his purples and vermillions. We passed Ailsa Crag before it was quite dark, but it was too late by that time for us to do it justice in a plate. However, we had succeeded in several distant views, so we had no cause to be discontented. As we passed the captain ordered the steam-whistle to be blown, which had the effect of sending up an innumerable cloud of sea-birds from their nests on the rock. For some minutes the air was simply alive with kittiewakes, gulls, solan geese, gannets, blackbacks, and other birds, whose screams and cries drowned every other sound. Then we steamed on, and the great Crag was left far astern until it was simply a dark loom in the darkness.

It was unanimously voted that it was simply preposterous to go to bed early on a night like this, when the water was rippling pleasantly and the moon silvering our decks. A proposition for a game of "Nap." was met with disdain as being too prosaic for the occasion, and an impromptu concert *al fresco* was declared to be the very thing. The captain joined in and brought the mate. The bagmen mustered in full force. Even the young ladies were induced to come on deck, and eventually one of them went so far as to sing a song – "Won't you tell me why, Robin?" – which was the hit of the evening. The captain also obliged the company, and, indeed, we all did our best to please, though, if the noises emitted by some of our party, including myself, pleased anyone, that person must have had a wonderful faculty for pleasure. They struck me at the time, I remember, as being very painful; however, the audience were lenient and a roaring chorus covers a multitude of sins. So we enjoyed ourselves to our hearts' content until nine bells, or some other heathenish hour unintelligible to landsmen, came to put an end to the festivity.

Next morning – a Tuesday, if I remember right – found us steaming into the Bay of Dublin with the long line of the Irish coast on each side of us, and a single hill in front which marked the position of the city. As we approached it we expended a couple of plates upon the scene; but Dublin from the seaside is neither picturesque nor impressive. Steaming up the Liffey we threw out our warps at the North Wall, and found that six hours would elapse before the unloading of the cargo and the state of the tide would allow us to pursue our journey. We spent this time in rambling over the Irish metropolis, and were surprised at the civility we met with and at the order of the streets. The newspapers had prepared us to find it in a state of semi-rebellion; but, as a matter of fact, everything was quiet enough. The only bad symptom we could see was the great number of big, hulking fellows lounging about without employment – "corner boys" they are named there – apparently ripe for any mischief.

The monotony of our voyage was relieved by our running high and dry upon a mud-bank in our attempt to leave the Liffey. This incident delayed us for two or three hours, so that it was late before we found ourselves at sea once more. We spent the night running down the Irish coast, and at six in the morning steamed past Dungannon and entered the mouth of the Waterford river, which winds along for many miles, and is so narrow that the sight of a large steamer upon it has a most incongruous effect. In our ascent of it we took several views of the wooded banks with country houses peeping here and there from among the trees. A sudden bend of the river brought us right up to the town – a long, thin straggling line of grey houses with a few steeples here and there, and a sprinkling of shipping in the river in front of it, the whole giving rather an impression of decay.

Bidding good-bye to our jovial captain we left the "Rathlin" with

sincere regret, having met with nothing but kindness and attention aboard of her. Our luggage was removed to the nearest hotel,
and we ourselves rambled with our cameras over the old town.
We were shown the spot where some English conqueror had
landed; though whether it was Cromwell or Richard Strongbow
seemed a mystery to our guide, and when questioned on the
subject he seemed to have a general idea that they were one and
the same person. We were also shown a hypothetical site where
the first potato planted upon Irish soil was supposed to have been
placed by Sir Walter Raleigh when he came over to hunt the
Ormond to death. As ardent potatophagi we all photographed
the place religiously, though I believe there are at least half-a-
dozen places in Ireland which claim the same distinction, among
which our ultimate destination, Youghal, claims a prominent
place.

We slept that night at Waterford, and set off the next day for
the above mentioned port. By the way, it was at Waterford that we
first began to see those seditious notices of which we had so often
read. Just opposite our steamer, I remember, as we came off
there was a tremendous placard imploring the citizens of the
county to assemble in their millions (the census returns only
account for about a hundred and fifty thousand), and to hold
their crops, whatever that might mean. We also saw the trad-
itional Irish peasant, whom I had always imagined to be a myth
invented for music-hall purposes. There he was, however, as
large as life, with corduroy knee-breeches, blue stockings, and a
high, soft hat with a pipe stuck in the side of it. The delusion was
so strong with us all, however, that we always had an inclination to
assemble round each one we met and wait for a song. Truly travel
enlarges men's minds.

Youghal is only a short distance from Waterford as the crow
flies, but it is a formidable journey by rail. However, even an Irish
train reaches its destination at last, and we found ourselves next
day in the old Irish seaport. Here the Blackwater river opens out
into a considerable estuary, which in turn opens out into the Irish
Sea. The town itself is a quaint, old-fashioned place, with an
amphibious population who live principally by fishing for the
salmon as they try to ascend the Blackwater, and capturing them
in long drift-nets.

The cousin of our friend Smith had been as good as his word,
and his yacht was waiting for us in the harbour, a fine, roomy,
old-fashioned craft, broad in the beam, with a cabin which would
hold the whole of us. She was well provided with nets and trawling
gear, the latter being a favourite amusement of her proprietor.

We only made an experimental cruise that day, standing off and on the land, outside the harbour. We got several excellent views of the town from the sea face, but others were complete failures; for we soon found the difference in working on the broad deck of a steamer and on a tossing little cockle-shell. On landing, however, we were amply recompensed by a series of views of the antiquities of the little place taken in the evening, after which we adjourned to a popular concert, where the chief hit seemed to be a topical song with frequent allusions to "Buckshot Forster," which never failed to bring down the house. We put up at the "Crown" Hotel, where we met with the greatest kindness and comfort, and can conscientiously recommend it to any other of the fraternity who may find themselves in that quarter.

Next morning with "a wet sheet and a flowing sea" – Cunningham suggested "a wet blanket" – we scudded out of Youghal harbour, threading our way amongst fishing boats and drift nets. There was a slight chopping sea on, which made photography almost an impossibility for the time; so all hands devoted themselves, heart and soul, to drinking bottled beer and trawling. The great net with its big iron sinkers, or "otters" as they are called, was lowered overboard and we dragged it behind us for half-an-hour or so. Our worthy host, who was an accomplished yachtsman, seemed considerably amused by our complete ignorance of boats and everything pertaining thereto. As Mark Twain said – the information which we did not possess would make a good-sized volume. Ramsay was the most erudite among us, but even he seemed to have a general impression that the flying jib was connected in some way with the tiller. "It's been out long enough now!" cried our skipper; "haul away at the line." We all began to haul away at various lines with desperate eagerness until by objurgation and example, he concentrated us upon the right one. There is an excited cry of "it's heavy – awfully heavy!" Up it comes through the blue water. We can see the bag of it flickering upwards, much distended apparently. "It's nothing but seaweed!" roars one. "I see a fish!" yells another. "Lots of them!" gasps a third. "Pull, boys, pull!" and then with a heavy splash down comes the net upon the deck, and next moment the whole place seems alive with flapping tails and waving fins and silver bellies and great red gills opening and shutting. It is a case of minding your ankles while a dogfish snaps at one side of the little deck and a conger eel both barks and bites at the other. However, all are successfully knocked on the head and we are able to classify our victims. There is a variety with a vengeance – hake, ling, rockcod, gurnard, red and grey mullet, eels, skate, crabs, octopi, the dogfish, and molluscs galore. Now was the time for photography to assert itself and come to the front. The net is piled tastefully in the sheets for a background; then with a little judicious selection a graceful and natural pile of fish are arranged in front, and we have a triumphal plate to remind us of our great haul.

We had several more "scrapes," as they are technically called, but none so successful as the first. Then we stood in well under the basaltic cliffs which line the coast, and which are hollowed out by the action of the waves. The water is calmer near the shore, and we succeeded in getting several very fair plates of these preci-pices, and of the fantastic gullies and fissures made in them by the action of the water.

By the afternoon we had worked round the rocky point which lies to the north of Youghal, and after passing several headlands had made our way into the beautiful bay of Ardmore, where we cast anchor and went ashore in the dinghy, taking, of course, our cameras with us.

It was fortunate we did so, for we never had a better oppor-tunity of getting some of those typical representations of Irish life which we had contemplated originally. Ardmore is a primitive village which has stood where it stands now for at least two thousand years without apparently altering very much one way or the other. It consists of a single line of whitewashed thatched cottages hung round with nets, and most of them possessing some sort of potato garden in the rear. These people really seem to have a grievance; for their bay is so exposed and the sea runs in with such violence that they are unable to have any boats except such as are light enough to be drawn ashore when the weather is threatening. Could they get the roughest and rudest breakwater it would be of enormous use to them; but they have no money of their own, and parliament has refused to advance them any, so fishing there is still exactly what it was when the ancient Britons went out in canoes with their rough nets. The people were a kindly, simple race, and looked on with much interest and delight while we took views of their houses and of their wives and families. They seemed to be in the last depths of poverty, but cheerful and cleanly, and very busy making ready for a descent of sprats which was expected every day.

Behind the village there is the most perfect specimen in Ireland of that mysterious edifice known as the round tower. This one was about seventy feet high, built very much like a modern lighthouse. Though its erection is entirely pre-historic, the mortar between the stones is as firm now as ever, and the stones themselves do not show the least symptoms of decay. We took several views of this interesting building. What the original object of the round towers was is a puzzle to antiquaries. Some have thought that they were temples erected in honour of the sun god; and this seems to have been the idea among the early Christians, for a church has been erected beside the tower, apparently to act as an antidote to it. The church, however, is now reduced to a crumbling ruin, while the old heathen tower is as erect and defiant as ever. Others have thought that they were watch towers, but that is negatived by the fact that this one is built at the foot of a hill, which would be rather an unnatural situation for a watch tower. Altogether the building and its uses were "the sort of thing no fellah would understand," so we contented ourselves with photographing it without indulging in further speculation.

We dined at the house of a hospitable medical man, and after dinner went over some of the other curiosities of this quaint, old place. Among these is the black stone of Ardmore, which is celebrated over the whole south of Ireland for its miraculous virtues. It is a meteoric stone with a large hole through the centre of it, and it is only on one day in the year that it possesses its strange powers. On that day the sick and lame of all the country round come down to the beach at Ardmore, and, forming a long line, they crawl in turn through the hole in the stone. Whether from the power of faith or the sea air or some other cause, many cures are said to result from this mode of treatment. Of course we all religiously took plates of this petrified physician.

We spent that night on board our yacht in Ardmore bay, and returned to Youghal in the morning. It had been our intention to run down the coast to Queenstown, but on coming back to our head-quarters we found a telegram waiting which summoned Ramsay back to Scotland on an urgent matter of business. Smith elected to accompany him, and the two left us for Waterford. As our little party was thus broken up we gave up our original plan, and on our hospitable captain inviting Cunningham and myself to come up the Blackwater with him and stay at his place for a week we very gladly availed ourselves of the invitation. What we saw and did in the Blackwater Valley I may reserve for another paper. Suffice it that the short excursion along the Waterford coast was a thoroughly enjoyable one, and that our only grief was that it should have been so curtailed.

A DAY ON "THE ISLAND"

————— ❖ —————

Perhaps there is no tract of land in the world which compresses into such a small space so many diversities of configuration as the Isle of Wight. It is a miniature of the great country from which it has been separated. There are moors and fells as bleak as those of Cumberland or the West Riding; chalk downs which recall Kent and Sussex; wooded undulating plains like those of Hampshire; and great stretches of rich arable land as fertile and as cultivated as any in Leicestershire. Amid such a variety of scenery, with the sea continually presenting itself as a background, and historical reminiscences upon every side, the amateur would be hard to please indeed who did not find subjects enough to gratify his photographic propensities.

In these days of rain and tempest, when outdoor photography is at a discount, and the ever-vigilant eye of the Astronomer-Royal fails to detect a ray of sunshine for weeks on end, there is a pleasure in recalling past campaigns with the camera, and hunting out from some secluded drawer batches of old prints of valley, fell, torrent and roadside inn, everyone of which recalls some pleasant companion or enjoyable excursion. But more profitable than these musings over bygone days is the pleasure of mapping out operations for the future. There must be many who are making preparations for the bright spring weather which will shortly be upon us, and to such a short sketch which may direct their attention to "fresh fields and pastures new" must be of interest. Let me endeavour, then, to give a brief description of what may be done within the limits of one day upon "The Island," as it is proudly called by its inhabitants, to the exclusion of all other islands upon the surface of the globe.

To my friend Johnson, of London, the path to the Isle of Wight lies through the Waterloo Station. Behold him there at an early hour of the morning, clad in a fearful and wonderful Ulster, and the slouched hat dear to the artistic and Bohemian mind. No need to inquire the object of his mission, for under his arm is his folded stand, and in his one hand he bears the most compressible of cameras, while the other is occupied with a handy deal box containing plates and necessaries. Johnson goes through the formality of paying fifteen shillings and receiving a return ticket to Ryde in exchange; and then, with a feeling that come what may his retreat is secured, is whirled off in a third-class carriage.

The journey to Portsmouth occupies about two hours and a-half, and the traveller is eventually deposited upon the harbour pier, alongside which the fine, roomy "Victoria" is snorting impatiently out of its two funnels, and in full readiness for its short voyage. There the Doctor, with apparatus corded and strapped, has been stamping up and down for a-quarter of an hour waiting for the London train.

From the quarter-deck of the "Victoria" a magnificent view of the harbour was to be obtained. There was a-quarter of an hour yet before the steamer could get the baggage aboard, and our photographers spied their opportunity. There was a clattering of straps, a turning of keys, a fitting of joints, and two uncouth three-legged, one-eyed creatures sprang into being. It was one of those bright, breezy mornings on which mere existence is a pleasure, and which gladden the heart of the photographer. A few bystanders gather curiously round, but the operators are imperturbable. The carrier is slipped in, the slide is slipped out, the shortest of exposures allowed, and the deed is done. Surely a more interesting view was never committed to gelatine. In the foreground lie three great three-deckers – the "Victory" (the old historical flagship of Nelson), the "Duke of Wellington," and the "St. Vincent." Beside these great floating monsters is moored a tiny gunboat – a representative of the modern tendency of naval architecture as compared with the ancient. By the side of its companions it looks like a duckling among swans; yet in its very insignificance lies its strength, since it offers no target for an enemy's shot. Around and between these vessels a swarm of steam launches, yachts, and shore boats fill in the scene, while behind it all the quaint little town of Gosport lines the water's edge and forms a background to the picture. Both plates were complete successes, giving as good an idea of the effect as can be produced without the blue of the sea, the grey of the houses, and the fluttering, coloured pennons of the men-of-war, with the artistic dash of brilliant scarlet from the coats of the marines upon the quarter-decks.

And now the good ship "Victoria" gives a final snort of expostulation, and churns up the water impatiently with her paddles. "All aboard!" shouts the captain. The warps are thrown off, and the vessel steams slowly out of the harbour, passing under frowning batteries, where the black-mouthed cannon peep sullenly out, as though sulky at having no more honourable task than the firing of salutes for so many hundreds of years. The channel here seems to the uninitiated to lie dangerously near the shore, even the largest ships passing within a stone's throw of the beach. There is a story, indeed, that on the occasion of some great wooden man-of-war going out in the beginning of the century she ran her bowsprit through the coffee-room window of the Blue Posts Hotel, considerably to the astonishment of some gentlemen who were dining therein. How far this is legendary and how far true is for some local historian to decide.

After touching at Southsea Pier the steamer stood right across for "the Island." Finer views could hardly be obtained than those of receding Southsea, with its charming variety of colour, white and red alternating in the houses, and the long line of shingle with the waves breaking merrily against it, or of the approaching shores of the Isle of Wight, with its undulating wooded hills, and the towers of Osborne peeping above the trees on the extreme right. Both were transferred to the plates of the photographers, together with a beautiful seascape of the Solent, with a solitary man-of-war lying at anchor at Spithead, and the three marine forts which stand out of the water like so many gigantic cheese-boxes, and command the winding channel which leads to the harbour. As the light was somewhat glaring the sky-shade was used in taking these views.

The Solent is five miles broad between Portsmouth and Ryde, so that twenty-five minutes of steaming brings the travellers across. Johnson's train has landed him on the pier at ten o'clock, and it is now hardly eleven, so that our excursionists have still a long day before them. Ryde pier is a very long one. As Johnson remarked, if it were a little longer there would be no need for any steamers at all. Happily there is a steam tramway which runs down it, and saves the necessity of trudging over half-a-mile of planking. The town itself is a decidedly hilly one. It is not so steep as the side of a house, but considerably more so than the roof. If you slip anywhere within half-a-mile or so you run a chance of reaching the beach in a shorter time than ever you took to traverse the same distance before. This is when you do not happen to bump into an inhabitant. In that case it is the inhabitant who gyrates down to the shore. If balloons were substituted for cabs in this town it would allow some small degree of comfort during the short time which will elapse before the whole thing goes adrift and slides majestically into the sea. I could say several ill-natured things of Ryde, but I refrain. A sense of my duty to the public, however, compels me to warn all future photographic travellers against every form of spirits in the island; for malignancy and venom they transcend anything I have ever imbibed, except, perhaps, the trade rum of Africa, which drunk raw out of a broken cocoa-nut shell, tastes like a torchlight procession.

To follow our travellers, however: the first move after getting into the town of Ryde is to repair to a large horse-and-trap agency there, and to engage an open carriage for the day – a matter which is not a very expensive one. Thus provided, the whole island is at their command. Should their tastes lie in the direction of Royalty, it is but six miles from the palace, where there are many beautiful views to be had; and just beyond lies the quaint old town of Cowes, with the many studies of the finest yachts in England which can be obtained there. If, however, the artist be of a historical and archaeological turn, then he should wend his way to the little town of Newport, the capital of the island, where, besides its many inherent beauties, there is the opportunity of viewing and photographing the venerable castle of Carisbrooke, in which Charles I was imprisoned before being taken to London and tried by the Parliament.

To confine myself to actual facts, however, the travellers, after a council of war with their driver, decided upon a somewhat more ambitious scheme than either of those indicated above. This was to drive right across the island, after first inspecting the Roman antiquities which have been lately unearthed at Brading. Brading is about four miles from Ryde, and as the road runs along the hills overlooking the sea the view was a beautiful one. Twice was the Doctor tempted out of the carriage and twice did splendid seascapes reward him; while Johnson, more improvident of plates and less accustomed to such scenery, excited the slumbering wrath of the driver by a long series of stoppages at the most inconvenient places – a wrath which showed itself in many mutterings and shruggings of shoulders, and was only eventually washed away by copious offerings of beer.

Brading is a pleasant little spot, and derives its principal importance from the magnificent specimen of a Roman villa which has been dug up in the immediate vicinity. From a short distance this interesting relic looks more like a quarry than anything else; and, alas! the operations of the photographer are confined to a distance, since the picturing of the tessellated pavement and other remains are a monopoly which the vagrant artist is not allowed to infringe upon. The tourists had to content themselves, therefore, with this general treatment of the subject, and then, after being divorced from their cameras, were led through the different chambers by a remorseless guide who explained the habits and customs of the "hancient Romans" in a manner which was more amusing than trustworthy.

The road from Brading leads to Newport, but there is a side road which opens into the highway between Ryde and Ventnor, and this was selected by the driver. This main road, which runs from north to south across the island, passes over a succession of undulating hills, from the summit of every one of which a magnificent view is to be obtained. Curious features on the scenery are the numerous monoliths – long perpendicular stones erected upon the summits of these hills, either as landmarks or for some other purpose. These abound in the Isle of Wight. A succession of little villages were passed through on the way, offering as fine a selection of rural "bits" as could be found anywhere – the little wayside cottage with thatched roof, diamond-paned windows, and clematis or Virginia creeper fringing the doorway; or, perhaps, the grizzled, round-shouldered proprietor, with his black pipe in his mouth, sitting "*sub tegmine fagi*," densely unconscious that he is about to be endowed with a franchise, and that the press of the country are clamouring about his wrongs. There is often more interest in a little scene of this sort, selected artistically and well worked out, than in the broadest and most ambitious rendering of the beauties of nature.

Ventnor is about twelve miles from Ryde. As you plunge into the heart of the country the sea disappears entirely, and you might imagine yourself in one of the midland counties of England. About three miles from Ventnor there is a large inn on one side of the road and a wicket gate on the other. Here the coachman pulls up with decision. At first, knowing the habits and customs of coachmen, our travellers imagine the inn to be the reason of this peremptory halt; but the landlord quickly sets them right, and they learn that the wicket gate is the attraction. Passing through it, camera in hand, they pick their way down a winding path and then across a brawling torrent. From there the path runs down a thickly-wooded valley, the trees meeting overhead so as to hide the sky, and the stream gurgling among the bracken far beneath. This is the famous Shanklin Chine, and certainly a more beautiful or fairy-like scene could hardly be conceived. The Londoner did it justice, however, in the two plates which he expended over it – a proceeding very jealously watched by the custodian of the place, who derives his income largely from the sale of prints.

Leaving the Chine behind, the carriage rolled over a tolerably-level road a couple of miles in length, terminating in a steep hill, which was rather a pull for the tired horse. Up to this, as I have said, there were no signs of the sea, but on reaching the crest of the hill a wonderful view lay before the party. Almost directly beneath was the ocean, stretching right away in every direction to the horizon. Coming so unexpectedly I know of no view in the world which gives such an idea of an infinite expanse. Here and there one looks straight down on the deck of some steamer or sailing ship, ploughing across to St. Malo or tacking along to Southampton. They look like toy vessels – mere specks in the enormous stretch of water around them. It is needless to say that cameras were once more in requisition, and this magnificent seascape packed away in our plate carriers.

When one leaves Ryde he fancies that he has seen the steepest town in the world, but his mind broadens when he comes to Ventnor. It is very much steeper, and gives the impression of being a little more than perpendicular. It is the fact of being built on the side of this hill that gives the place its great reputation as a resort for consumptives. No wind but the balmy south one can get near it. Still there are draw-backs, and when a consumptive falls out of his front door down the High-street and into the sea his language is just as virulent as that of any healthy man.

Commend me to the "Crab and Lobster" Hotel at Ventnor. Its situation is charming, its fare excellent, and its charges moderate; or, at least, moderate for the island, which is never at any time an economical spot. At one of the open windows which line the elegant coffee-room, and through which the summer breeze wafts the perfume of many a flower unknown in higher latitudes, there sat that day two pampered and enervated photographers who had solemnly packed away their cameras and delivered their whole minds up to the one idea of a comfortable dinner with a soothing pipe to follow. After all they had a right then to indulge in a little *dolce far niente*, since they had accumulated a finer variety of picturesque effects and interesting views than could have been taken in a week in a less-favoured locality.

It was necessary for the Doctor to be back in Southsea by nightfall, and the Londoner was also determined to be back in town by the evening train, so that after a climb over the curious little town the carriage was discarded and the train taken back to Ryde. Here the six o'clock boat was caught, and by seven the professional man was among his patients, and his friend within two hours was striding once more along the platform at Waterloo – a poorer man by some two pounds, but a richer one by the varied assortment of artistic pictures which he bore in his little deal box, as well as by the store of iodine and ozone which had renovated his lungs and oxidised the carbon of London.

In this little sketch I have simply attempted to give some idea of the pleasure and instruction which may be compressed into a single day by dint of a little energy and enterprise. A few such excursions during the summer months would, without being any great drag upon his purse, teach him with a splendid series of pictures. If there be any one of my readers whose attention is drawn by this short article to the magnificent field of outdoor work presented by the Isle of Wight, then I have not written in vain.

EASTER MONDAY WITH THE CAMERA

—————◆—————

Portsmouth is never at any time a dull place. The coming and going of men-of-war and of transports, the large garrison, the crowds of "blue jackets," and the annual fashionable influx into Southsea – all prevent its ever becoming so. When the town is *en fête*, however, and puts up her triumphal arches, decks herself with gay ribbons, and assumes her other coquettish airs, she is as lively as any Spanish city in carnival time. Those who had the good fortune to see her last Easter will not readily forget her attractions.

From Saturday to Monday the main streets of the borough were a gay spectacle. Above, every variety of flag and banner were festooned across from house to house, or fluttered from window or roof. Mottoes, devices, and illuminations glittered and glanced on every side. The pavements were crowded with uniforms. Blue marines and red marines, linesmen and dragoons, royal artillery and blue jackets, volunteer artillery and engineers, spruce London Scottish and grey Artists, riflemen, black, blue, red and grey from the metropolitan corps – all swarmed and jostled and pushed from one end of Commercial Road to the other. Very serviceable the citizen soldiers looked, with bayonet and water bottle, blanket and haversack – ready apparently to go anywhere and do anything, more particularly to drink. Considering that on Saturday night there were some fifteen thousand men in the town order was wonderfully well preserved. There was only one disturbance of any consequence which I observed, where some regular engineers having given offence to a few volunteers a free fight ensued, in which a couple of sailors joined, fighting apparently like Hal of the Wynd – each for his own hand and with the strictest impartiality. In this skirmish the volunteers had decidedly the best of it, and remained in possession of the field.

Easter Monday morning broke bleak and raw, and it became a

problem of some difficulty to know how camera and stand and carriers were to be conveyed to the top of the Portsdown ridge, some three and a-half miles from the town. Vehicles were at famine prices, and even the 'bus companies had run up their fares in a way which prompted all public-spirited citizens to "boycott" them. As my two companions and myself included ourselves in this category we proceeded to put our principles into practice – a resolution which led to sore heels, blisters, and much dust and exasperation. As far as we can learn, our abstention had not any perceptible effect upon the market value of 'bus shares. We have given up "boycotting" large companies since then.

Trudging along three miles of very dusty road with a camera in one's hand is not the most blissful of human employments, more particularly when the crowd upon the footpaths the whole way is so thick that you have to regulate your pace by that of others. You tread on the heels of those in front of you, and while they are expressing their opinion of you and of your proceedings in flowery and scriptural language, you are yourself trodden on by those behind. Vehicles of every sort and description clattered along the causeway, and as no rule of the road appeared to be observed it was dangerous to go off the footpath for a moment.

The lines of Hilsea having been passed, the first sign of warlike operations became visible in the shape of a pontoon bridge thrown across the canal by the engineers to allow the garrison to make their sortie. A little further on in a bye-road there stood a commissariat waggon of the London Scottish, with a guard of half-a-dozen men smoking round their stacked rifles – a pretty little warlike "bit" for the photographer; but the hurrying, re-morseless crowd prevented any possibility of taking it. We were glad to reach the prettily-decorated village of Cosham, and gladder still to get a glass of bitter beer, for we were coated with dust and as dry as if we had swallowed Paley's *Evidences of Christianity*.

The battle was to begin at twelve o'clock, and as we were anxious not to miss any of the slaughter we made a forced march so as to get on the ridge before that hour. There is not a finer natural theatre in the world than the Portsdown hill and the country around it, nor any place where such a large number of spectators can follow operations upon a large scale and grasp the drift of them. On one side beneath you is the village of Cosham and the little town of Portchester, with its historical castle, and on each side the broad stretches of Portsmouth harbour and Langstone harbour. In the background lies the great Hampshire seaport itself, and beyond it the silver streak of the Solent,

bounded on the horizon by the long, well-wooded shores of the
Isle of Wight. On the other side the declivity is as sharp, and the
spectator looks down on an undulating, fairly open country,
rolling away for some twelve miles to Butser Hill and the Peters-
field district. The main roads stand out like lines of chalk – as,
indeed, many of them are – upon the landscape. Both views, to
the north and to the south, make splendid photographs, but we
had already done them justice and were in quest of rarer game.

To understand anything about the manœuvres it was necessary to have a highly-trained imagination. To grasp them thoroughly argued an immense power of fancy, only to be obtained,
as one of my companions declared, by the aid of stimulants. The
great forts which line the summit of the ridge, and command the
country round for miles, are to be supposed not to exist. This is
out of consideration for the wives and families of the invading
army. Then the sea is also abolished and put out of the question.
For the day Portsmouth was an inland town, defended by a
garrison of some two thousand men. A reinforcement of four
thousand or so are on their march from the westward to strength-
en the place. An enemy, however, numbering ten thousand or so,
comes down from the north in a highly-reprehensible and vindictive manner, and interposes itself between the town and the
relieving column, and endeavours to prevent its getting into the
town. This was the cause of all the trouble.

Looking down at the wooded country to the north and west it
was difficult to believe that some fifteen thousand troops were
within a radius of a few miles. The mystic hour of twelve arrived,
and whereas we civilians had fondly imagined that that moment
would be the signal for a roar of firing, for bidden troops to rush
out of ambuscades, and for a general lively time, to our intense
disappointment nothing whatever occurred. The landscape was
as placid as before, and not a human being to be seen in the north
valley except an occasional staff officer or umpire galloping
furiously along.

Presently a couple of Middlesex Yeomanry, with their carbines
unslung, came trotting along the ridge, followed by twenty or
thirty of the same corps. These were the extreme advance guard
of the northern force. Almost at the same moment a brass-
helmeted body of men, looking like a mounted fire brigade, came
galloping up from the other direction. These were the scouts of
the western army. There was the material for a pretty little cavalry
skirmish, and the crowd's flesh began to creep; but no gore was
shed, for the Middlesex men scampered back to their supports
and the Hampshires dismounted and occupied some broken

ground in mounted infantry fashion. We tried a plate over this manœuvering of cavalry, but it was not a success. The dim weather necessitated a somewhat long exposure, and it was no easy matter to keep our camera on its legs, or to get a clear foreground in front of the lens.

By this time there was a glitter of arms away to the eastward, and column after column of troops – black, grey, and red – appeared in sight marching up the valley, with a double line of skirmishers in front of the leading brigade. This was the attacking force. Their advance was directed towards the relieving or western army, but a rattle of musketry in the distance showed that the garrison had made a *sortie* and were engaging the flank of the invaders. At the same moment the head of the western force began to appear near Fort Southwick, and very shortly the skirmishers of both sides were hard at work. The sight in the valley now was a pretty one. Two long lines of smoke showed the position of the hostile skirmishers. Behind these on both sides were regiments hurrying up in open order to join in the fray; behind that again was the main body coming up in columns of companies, while the cavalry, finding the situation becoming somewhat warm, were slowly retiring. We would have found it impossible owing to the crush to have done any good work was it not for the kindness of a sergeant of mounted engineers, which corps was keeping the ground. Seeing our difficulty, he very kindly allowed us to come outside the line of demarcation, and so to work without having the apparatus broken or being elbowed off our legs. In this way we succeeded in getting a series of plates of the proceedings; but, as I have said, the weather was against any very brilliant results.

In the meantime there were terrible doings in the valley. The fighting line of both sides had been strongly reinforced, until it had absorbed the greater portion of either army. These two long lines were blazing away at each other with the greatest *sang-froid*, at distances which varied from fifty yards to two hundred. Occasionally a regiment would rise and make a rush forward or backward in a way which would have entailed a premature interview with their Creator had it been done in actual warfare. The reckless hardihood of these men was almost incredible. They were too brave to lie down, so they strutted about regardless of rifles and Nordenfeldts, with a cool contempt of danger which came like a revelation upon one of my companions, who had seen some real hard fighting in his lifetime, and who bore in his waistcoat pocket a certain piece of bronze called the Victoria Cross – as honestly earned as ever a decoration was. "Why," he remarked, "there wouldn't have been any of them left at all. They would have been utterly annihilated;" and we forthwith began planning out graveyards and arranging for the decent interment of the belligerents.

So far we had, all things considered, no reason to be dissatisfied with our day's work from a photographic point of view. When the "cease firing" sounded, however, and the march past was about to begin, we found the crowd so dense about the saluting point that photography was not only out of the question, but it was absolutely necessary for us to abandon our apparatus if we wished to see anything ourselves. Handing it over, therefore, to the care of a friendly sutler, we elbowed our way through the crowd – there must have been more than a hundred thousand people on the side of the hill – and eventually secured a position not very far from the staff, where were the Duke of Cambridge, Prince Edward of Saxe-Weimar, the popular Governor of Portsmouth, and many others of light and leading, including the French military *attaché* – a gaudy warrior in red trousers and sky-blue coat, who seemed, to judge by his expression, to think very small beer of our citizen army.

The march past began with the scanty force of yeomanry, and then for rather over an hour regiment followed regiment until the whole had gone by, some of the principal ones being cheered by the crowd. The local Hampshire corps, some eight hundred strong, went by in the opinion of experts in better style than any of the metropolitan regiments, which may be explained by the fact that belonging to a military town they have constant opportunities of imitating and competing with the regulars. The Victorias, the Artists, the London Irish and Scotch, the West-minsters, the Second Sussex Artillery, the Inns of Court, and the Tower Hamlets all did well. The Nordenfeldts – grim-looking machines, pulled along in the rear of the Victoria Rifles – created considerable curiosity among the crowd. "What's them?" asked one fellow near us. "Them's the regimental cookin' apparatus," another answered, with a look of superior wisdom. "For cooking the enemy's goose," we ventured to suggest, but that joke fell upon barren ground and was lost. Taking them all in all the general opinion seemed to be that, though there were a good many weedy men in the ranks, the average of physique was very fair – undoubtedly superior to that of most of the present short-service regiments.

There was one episode in the fight upon Saturday which was somewhat amusing. Among the defenders there was a troop of the 4th Dragoon Guards – the heroes of the Kassassin charge –

and these slashing horsemen took a great delight in chasing and chevying any of the opposing yeomanry who came near them, thinking, no doubt, that it was capital fun to take a "rise" out of these amateur soldiers. One innocent-looking yeoman, after this game had been going on some time, rode straight towards the dragoons, and then, as if surprised at finding himself in the jaws of the lion, turned and fled. Away clattered the whole troop in hot pursuit, and rode right into a nice little ambuscade prepared by the Westminster Rifles, where they were all made prisoners. The innocent-looking yeoman had been a decoy duck, and the crest-fallen dragoons rode back, sadder and wiser men.

With the conclusion of the march past the proceedings terminated, and the various regiments began to file off the ground in different directions.

Our sutler had moved off with his cart containing the camera and carriers, and it took an hour's seeking before we discovered him. However, at last we unearthed the delinquent and recovered our invaluables, after which we turned our backs on the battle-field, where the carrion crow was already flapping its heavy wings over the empty ginger-beer bottles, and struck out for home.

Just outside Cosham we overtook an omnibus, which, for a wonder, was not full. We said nothing, but looked at each other. Should we be partners in bolstering up this monopoly – this indefensible overcharge? We had spent the last week in denouncing it. Were we to submit to it now? We got inside the 'bus while we were turning the question over in our minds, and arrived at Portsmouth before we had been able to come to any definite conclusion.

ARRAN IN AUTUMN

The island of Arran may be said to be the epitome of the whole of Scotland, just as the Isle of Wight is an England in miniature. Within the narrow bounds of Arran – it is some ten miles across and from fifteen to twenty in length – there is every variety of scenery. There are smiling lowlands and rugged highlands, wild woods, and barren heaths. Nowhere can the wandering photographer find in such a small compass so many varying beauties upon which to exercise his skill, and it is an important matter that members of the fraternity should know of such places. I know from my own experience that among amateurs who are fond of outdoor work many are engaged in business or professions, and it is difficult for them to get away for more than a very few days at a time. With such headquarters as Arran it is possible for them to compress into a short period as much valuable work as could be done in treble the time in a place the beauties of which were more scattered.

Having made up our mind for a holiday, and chosen Arran as the scene of our labour, my friend and I consumed the "midnight oil" in poring over guide-books and *Bradshaws* in order to get some information as to how we were to reach our destination. Let me publish the result of our researches, in case anyone should follow in our footsteps. The first stage, then, is to get to Glasgow. From Glasgow one must travel by train to a small port named Ardrossan, the distance being about twenty miles. Ardrossan is situated exactly opposite the island, and steamers ply between two or three times a day to the two chief centres of Arran – Brodick and Lamlash.

My friend was of a statistical and economical turn of mind. "We ought to do it on three pound ten each," he remarked. "Put it down at a 'fiver,' " I suggested. "Fiver be hanged!" he roared, with the indignation of an outraged financier. "How can you spend five pounds if you are moderately careful? A return ticket to Glasgow won't cost more than thirty shillings, if you choose your time. Trains to Ardrossan (say) four shillings the return, and the boat to Arran you may put at another four shillings. Thirty-eight shillings for travelling." "Cabs," I suggested, in a still, small voice. "Well; say two pounds five all included," continued the Chancellor of the Exchequer. "Then there is our board and lodging in a cottage for three days. What else is there?" "Casual drinks," I replied. "Let us have one," said the wearied economist, and we relapsed.

With our hands full of gear then, and our heads full of figures, we found our way to Glasgow, travelling during the night so as to catch the early train for Ardrossan. There is a boat which waits for this train, so that we had no time to wait in the quaint little Scottish port, but found ourselves and belongings within five minutes upon the deck of a smart little steamer, and in another five minutes were steaming out of the harbour in company with forty or fifty fellow passengers.

The view of Arran as one approaches it is magnificent. A ring of yellow sand runs round the greater portion of the island, behind which rise up sloping green braes and dark fir forests. Behind these again are the rugged group of mountains, which form the north and centre of the island, the whole culminating in the majestic Goatfell, which towers up to nearly three thousand feet. The mist of morning was still rising, and the sunlight upon it gave the mountains that peculiar purple tinge which is characteristic of highland scenery, and which Horatio McCullough and Waller Paton knew so well how to imitate. It might have been some enchanted island which floated upon the calm azure sea. Behind us was the long line of the Scottish coast, with the one great gap which indicated the mouth of the Clyde, and away to the north the long jagged ridge of the Argyleshire hills. To the south stretched the Irish sea, broken only by the tall, white dome-like summit of Ailsa Craig, the strange solitary rock which stands out like a gigantic Druidical monolith amid the waste of waters.

Any romantic feelings which may have been aroused by the appearance of Arran were rudely dispelled by the demand for twopence each from the official who guards the pier at Brodick, and levies a tax upon all invaders. "Every prospect pleases and only man is vile," my friend quoted, as we trudged along the road which leads from the pier to the little township. There is a very fair hotel there, but we had determined to put up at a cottage kept by Mrs. Fullarton, with whom some friends of ours had boarded upon a previous occasion. We were aware that this good woman lived somewhere in the vicinity of Brodick, but we had lost her exact address. "Can you tell me where any one of the name of Fullarton lives?" we asked an aged islander. The veteran smiled pensively. It appears from his statement that the whole population of the island are, with some few exceptions, all called "Fullarton." Eventually, however, by an ingenious cross-examination, and a happy recollection on the part of my friend that the woman in question had a lame leg, we succeeded in obtaining directions which led us to a little farmhouse, which proved to be the abode of the individual whom we were in search of.

Anyone who ventures into Arran must be prepared to rough it in the matter of edibles. Meat is a rare and scarce commodity. Bacon and eggs can generally be relied on, and fish are usually to be had. There are plenty of potatoes, and with a little butter the traveller can generally manage to arrange a succulent and nutritious meal without the aid of a butcher. Prices are extremely reasonable, and our board and lodging – we had a large room, which combined sitting-room and bedroom – only cost us a few shillings a day.

We had arranged to make no very long excursions upon the next day, but contented ourselves with wandering down to the village with our cameras, and as it was a beautifully bright morning we were rewarded by several excellent places. The broad stretch of Brodick Bay, with the Scotch coast in the background, formed a beautiful seascape, and the inland view, including the magnificent castle of the Duke of Hamilton, which peeps from among the trees at the base of the hills, was equally effective.

In the afternoon we wandered along the seashore as far as the little fishing hamlet of Corrie, some five miles from Brodick. The whole distance was one suggestion of magnificent "bits," had we only had plates enough to do them justice. As it was, our carriers were soon filled, and we abandoned our gear at a fisherman's cottage, and picked it up again on our return. From Corrie a grand view is to be seen of the mountains and beautiful glens of Glen Sannox and Glen Ross, which intervene between them.

A local curiosity was pointed out to us in the shape of a rock called the "Giant's Harp," on account of some resemblance which it was supposed to bear to the instrument. As a matter of fact, anything more elaborately unlike a harp it would be impossible to conceive. There used to be a rocking boulder in this neighbourhood, which, although it weighed several tons, was so delicately balanced that the slightest pressure would cause it to rock backwards and forwards. An officer and some seamen from a man-of-war, however, levered it over into the sea one day, for which piece of senseless Vandalism they were, I am glad to say, heavily mulct in a lawsuit taken against them by the islanders, on the ground that they had deprived them of one of the attractions which used to draw tourists to the place. After a most pleasant and profitable day we returned to our farm, and agreed over our evening pipe that it was a pity that we had not three weeks instead of three days to devote to the island and its beauties.

Next day we were up betimes, and made the pleasing discovery that there were two stout hobbledehoys attached to the establishment, who were ready for a small consideration to carry our *impedimenta* in any given direction for any given time. With these retainers in our rear we set off for a walk across the island. The path was desolate enough, running over a barren heathercovered heath, with an occasional gaunt telegraph post to break the monotony. We were rewarded, however, when we reached the other side by some beautiful scenery. It was an exceptionally clear day, and we could distinctly see the north end of Ireland, lying like a dark line upon the water. The chief object of curiosity was a cave, which is pointed out as being the one in which King Robert the Bruce observed the manœuvres of the persevering but weak-minded spider, which endeavoured to swarm up a thread when it ought to have crawled up the wall.

This and several other points of interest were done justice to, as also was the lunch which we had had the foresight to bring with us and which we and our camp followers discussed amicably together by the side of a little brook which runs down into the sea. We photographed the spot afterwards, including in the picture our two aboriginies, who have been since, I hear, greatly pleased and astonished at receiving a print each as a momento of the occasion. Then, as our plates were once more exhausted as well as our provisions, we turned our heads eastward, and, after a long but pleasant walk, found ourselves once more at our modest head-quarters. We had converted one of our landlady's spacious cupboards into a dark room, and were able, that evening, to satisfy ourselves as to the success of most of our results. All those which we developed were excellent.

A curious incident occurred during the night. Our sleep was disturbed by a strange noise on the thatched roof above our bedroom, as of some heavy object moving about. At last we flung open the window, on which a man slid down the sloping roof and fled down the road. In the morning we found that he had actually removed part of the thatch, evidently with the intention of boring a way into our chamber. What his motives were we could never discover; but probably the purses of Sassenach strangers were the chief incentives to his enterprise. Our landlady put him down as an Irish harvester, many of whom had lingered about the island after their services had ceased to be wanted.

The next day was the last and the most important of our little holiday. We had determined to ascend Goatfell – a feat which seemed a great thing to my companion, who had done little mountaineering in the course of his life. We started at about seven in the morning, after a substantial porridge breakfast, with our two faithful followers bearing our camera-cases and plate-carriers. We ourselves were burdened with knapsacks containing provisions for the day. The morning was bright, but a chilliness in the air warned us that summer had fled. As we emerged from the forests of the Duke of Hamilton (in which the red deer swarmed upon every side, and climbed the sloping uplands beyond) the view was a marvellous one. From Bute and the Mull of Cantire, in the north almost as far as Wigtonshire, in the south the whole coast line of Scotland lay revealed. Down beneath us the blue ocean was flecked with the white sails of yachts and fishing boats, while here and there a dark cloud showed where some great steamer was ploughing its way to the great Scotch seaport.

We expended a couple of plates – one of which was afterwards unfortunately ruined by fogging – upon the scene, and then turning to our task, continued to clamber up the mountain. The declivity is not very steep until the last few hundred yards when it becomes almost precipitous, but we managed, thanks to our young islanders, to convey not only ourselves but our instruments also in safety to the summit. To the north the country seemed a very abomination of desolation – a world of wild peaks, of rugged chasms, and brown gnarled rocks, all inextricably jumbled together. I have been up several of the Alps, but have never seen a grander mountain view than is to be seen from the summit of Goatfell. The Carline's Leap, a great double-peaked mountain, within a few hundred feet of the same height as the one on which we stood was the nearest of the rocky family. It derives its name, as one of our youths informed us, from the fact that there is a legend in the island which sets it down as the site of a witch's revel or Walpurgis' Nacht, and it is said that on certain nights the old sinners are still to be seen mounted upon the conventional broomstick and skimming across from one peak to the other.

Having had our luncheon upon the summit, and smoked a pensive pipe while we admired the great panorama before us, we erected our cameras and took several pictures each, most of which turned out satisfactorily. By that time the afternoon was far gone and it was only by hard walking that we succeeded in accomplishing the descent and reaching Brodick before night fell. A dreamless sleep rewarded us after our unwonted exertions and rested our weary limbs.

It was with unfeigned regret that we took our leave next day of the beautiful island and its primitive inhabitants. Our few days there were most interesting to us both as photographers and as holiday seekers. If any member of the fraternity should ever desire a holiday which shall combine economy, amusement, and magnificent open-air studies, he cannot do better than follow in our footsteps. I may mention, as a conclusion, that my friend's modest estimate of the expense proved to be only a very little below the actual sum required.

WITH A CAMERA ON AN AFRICAN RIVER

———————◆———————

The great ship is lying at her anchor in the Calabar River, and the groaning of her chains and the whizzing of her steam-winches as she hoists the hogsheads of palm-oil on board show that her loading is not yet done. What can the idlers and passengers do, then? Why not explore, a little higher up, the mysterious pea-soup-coloured stream, and, since a camera is to be had, take a few plates, which may be of interest in days to come?

It needs but a word to the amiable captain, and the thing is done. Down goes the gig with a splash into the water. Her crew of red-capped, copper-faced Kroomen clamber like monkeys down the falls, and then sit like swarthy Apollos with the long oars in their dark sinewy hands. The camera is handed into the stern; its owner and his companions follow, and push off from the high black hull; four blades dip simultaneously into the water; and the long, thin boat speeds swiftly on its way.

The popular notion of a West African river is not usually associated with beauty. The fever and the miasma have given an evil reputation to those deadly streams, and their very name calls up visions of decaying vegetation and of malarious swamps. Yet in the coolness of the early morning there was much that was beautiful in the luxuriant foliage which skirted the banks and the tangle of palm trees which formed a background in every direction.

Opposite us in the town of Old Calabar, a confused assemblage of brown thatched native huts, and just along the water's edge a row of whitewashed factories in which the European agents do their business. Hills, all clad in feathery foliage, rise up behind the town. It is worth a plate now, for at this early hour there is some hope of a soft effect. A little later and the glaring sun will admit only those of chalky and hard effects which mar so many tropical pictures.

As we row lazily upstream there is much on either bank which would furnish a pretty and interesting picture. Here is a great mangrove tree with its hundred sinuous roots – a vegetable patriarch which has flourished there for generations. There on that muddy bank is a great crocodile basking in the morning sun. We turn our camera on him and are about to perpetuate his charms, but he looks up, sees what he no doubt considers to be the latest invention in fire-arms turned in his direction, and at once shuffles off into the yellow stream. Birds of the most beautiful colours, and butterflies almost as large as the birds, dart above and across our course, like flashes of coloured lightning. No doubt when the photographic millenium has come we shall be able to take these too, and to reproduce all their native brilliancy. At present we could but watch and wish.

Here is an island in mid-stream; a fluffy, feathery, palmtree-bearing island, on which some fever-proof Paul and Virginia might have taken up their abode. It is as pretty a "bit" as could be desired and we take it *en passant*. Even as we take the cap from the lens a solemn old pelican emerges from the bushes, like some quaint *genius loci*, and includes himself in the picture.

We have another characteristic group now in a dozen or more canoes coming down the stream with merchandise for Calabar. Their occupants with their dark childish smiling faces make an excellent study. Behind them comes the larger canoe of some chief. A priest in the bows waves a miniature broom from side to side, by means of which the evil spirits are supposed to be swept out of the great man's way. His lordship sits very complacently under an awning in the sheets of the boat, and the canoemen under his august eye bend sturdily to their strokes.

And now our appetite reminds us that, interesting as all this may be, the sight of our breakfasts would be more so still. The tide and stream aid our homeward journey and within an hour we are seated round the hospitable board of the *Mayumba*. Perhaps, some day in England, looking over our portfolio we may acknowledge that that morning was spent to advantage.

"A NEW SCIENTIFIC SUBJECT"

LETTERS TO THE EDITORS

———————— ❈ ————————

GENTLEMEN, – Mr. Wm. Brooks, in a recent number of the
JOURNAL, has started an interesting subject in the apparently
unaccountable things he relates in his experiments under the
head of *Effects of Contact or Pressures on the Sensitive Salts of Silver*,
and I agree with him in thinking that magnetism has an important
bearing on the subject; because it will be found upon investigation
that all bodies – especially such as are magnets, crystals, man, and
even the light of the sun and heavenly bodies – are polarised, and
that the light given forth by various bodies is not the same throughout, but that in polarised bodies, such as I have mentioned, one of
the poles would be orange or yellow, while the other would be of a
greyish-blue.

In the case of an experiment tried in Germany many years ago
the hands of a person shone with different lights, the left hand
appearing brighter, more distinct, and of a reddish-yellow, while
the right hand was blue and less clearly defined, a certain polarity
of colouring being thus manifested. Some persons are more
sensitive to this influence than others, and those that are, on
placing their hands over the poles of a magnet or crystal at a
distance of from one to three inches, perceive very particular
sensations, resembling sometimes those resulting from a tepid
breath, and sometimes that of a cold breath, in distinguishing
which they are not deceived, but obtain the same results at every
fresh trial.

Scientific men have discovered that from all objects having life
proceeds a force, to which they have given the name of "Od.,"
which may be explained thus, and which is an entire explanation
of the instances mentioned by Mr. Brooks in his paper. This was
studied by me some twelve years ago, and I now quote from my
note-book:– From our earth radiates an atmosphere called by
men of science a "photosphere," or luminous halo. From this

photosphere is thrown off another, called a "chromosphere" from its shedding forth rays of colour. Now from everything animate or inanimate on this earth is also shed forth rays of colour after its kind which affect the sensitive plate, and more especially the gelatine-bromide plate, in a greater or lesser degree, according to its intensity and its colour; and photography reveals to us the fact that in certain conditions of *body* each one of us has radiating from us a halo of light in greater or lesser proportion, varying in intensity according to our health and to the purity and impurity of our bodies. Women often having it stronger than men. Flowers also give forth light in the same manner, hyacinths expecially, their perfume conveying the fact to us, such being invisible particles of matter floating in the air immediately surrounding the particular flower. All this is easy of proof, as must be apparent to any well-ordered mind. Even in the matter of our daily clothing and hygiene, those who keep the body scrupulously clean find that it conduces to health, goodness of sight and hearing. Strength of limb and cleanliness and purity also conduce to an abundance of "Od." Those who have this force specially love the colour blue, disliking the colour yellow, whilst others like yellow, red, blue, yellow and red being in excess.

I have before spoken of the phenomena of sensation in similarity to the varying kinds of breath. In these is also manifested the same sort of dualism which has already been before noticed in the luminous emanations. *The right side of every person of either sex is cooler than the left side*, and from this we learn that man from the right to the left is polarised like crystals; and so also may be accounted for the seeming impossibility of Mr. Brooke's friend being able to develope his plates without fogging. His odic rays in some way affected the sensitive surface of the plate he was working.

But, to bring these odic impressions more especially within the experimental range of ourselves, I would add that they are either disagreeably warm or agreeably cool. This may readily be tried by any two persons, the hand or the foot (without shoe but with stocking on) of the one party held up, while the other makes passes with his hands on both or either side of the limb; after a few moments an agreeable cold sensation (it was so in my case) was felt which increased when continued for a long time. Moreover, on every occasion there may be observed an uneasiness at meeting with certain similar colours. I have noticed also the same with certain persons, namely, great and intense pleasure at meeting others, and an uneasiness at encountering dissimilar ones. For instance: a right hand shines with a blue light when approached to the blue pole of a magnet or crystal, while the right hand of another person feels an impression of repugnant warmth. The same is the case in respect to a left hand; whilst the left hand approached to blue light objects and the right approached to yellow objects gives, without exception, the impression of a delicious coolness. Hence it may be concluded that the poles of the same in magnets and crystals, as also the hands of men and women, are endowed with similar or reciprocally opposite properties, and that these constitute a dualism of great importance which plunges deep into all nature. In the very early numbers of *Chambers's Edinburgh Journal* may be found much upon this interesting subject.

In conclusion: I would add that even the most sombre colours are accompanied by scattered rays of white light in quantity amply sufficient to affect the sensitive film, and so from ourselves and from the glorious landscape that surrounds us also are shed forth rays of colour, each tree, shrub, flower, and earth giving forth its own ray of light, a *ray specially its own*, all derived from that great source of light – God himself. With these thoughts I leave the matter; only adding that I have succeeded in photographing a plant in its natural colours, and that I am still pursuing my experiments.

W. HARDING WARNER.

P.S. – In the specimen photograph enclosed, the colour in the geraniums, the tree ferns, the Indian-rubber plant with shining leaves and other plants, are more clearly seen by some persons than others. Even the delicate pink of the fuchsia has been seen by some. – W.H.W.

[The photograph enclosed is one of ordinary appearance, and neither we ourselves nor anyone to whom we have shown it has succeeded by any stretch of imagination in imparting the faintest idea of colour to it. – Editors of THE BRITISH JOURNAL OF PHOTOGRAPHY.]

GENTLEMEN, – I read with some interest and considerable surprise an article which appeared, under the above heading, in THE BRITISH JOURNAL OF PHOTOGRAPHY last week. I then read it again. After a short lapse of time, and a medical examination which reassured me as to the state of my intellect, I perused it for the third time; but I felt it would be a tempting of Providence to go deeper into the matter. Will Mr. Harding Warner consent to throw a "photosphere or luminous halo" round this Delphic utterance of his? Or are we to understand that it is a colossal practical joke which leaves in the shade Artemus Ward's description of the silver mine?

Mr. Warner cites as facts things which are incorrect, and that in a crisp and epigrammatic way which is delightful. From these so-called facts he draws inferences which, even if they were facts indeed, would be illogical, and upon these illogical inferences draws deductions which, once more, no amount of concession would render tenable. Let us for curiosity's sake brace ourselves for a mental effort, and wade along in Mr. Warner's trail, in the hope of picking up some little scrap of meaning.

Mr. Warner begins by the pretty broad assertion that "all bodies – especially such as are magnets, crystals, man [!], and even the light of the sun and heavenly bodies – are polarised." There may be some arguments as to how far such bodies may be polarised – though I believe that in physics the term is only applicable to light – but the use of the present tense and the offhanded looseness of the remark makes the sentence sound more like an extract from a nightmare of Professor Tyndall's than a sober scientific statement. There follows an incoherent allusion to "the polarity of colour" (whatever that may mean) and an account of some sensitive subjects who on placing their hands over "the poles of a crystal" were sensible of a "tepid breath," by which, I presume, the gentleman means a warm current of air – a curious circumstance, if true, but without the smallest bearing upon the subject at issue, if there can be said to be any subject at issue.

Mr. Warner then runs off upon another tack, and we might quote the bard that "this is a more beautiful song than the other." He tells us that scientific men have discovered a force in all living

things which they have named "Od." What scientific men? At the
risk of being flippant I should submit that it is very odd that such a
force should be mentioned in no text-book of science. Can it be
that the all-comprehensive syllable of the Hindoos, "Om" (if I
remember right), is running in the gentleman's mind? He is an
authority upon the subject, and favours us with a few jottings
which he made in his note-book some twelve years ago. After
running over a few rudiments of science, everyday common-
places, such as that there are two envelopes round the earth, one
emitting light and named a "photosphere," and the other "shedding forth rays of colour" named a "chromosphere" – both facts
guaranteed by "men of science" – he brings us to something a
little more off the beaten track. By virtue of "Od," says the
note-book, all things animate and inanimate emit rays of colour
which affect the sensitive plate, and more especially the gelatine-
bromide plate. Unfortunately for the credit of the note-book,
gelatine-bromide plates did not exist twelve years ago. But, apart
from this minor consideration, was ever such an extraordinary
statement promulgated in a scientific journal? Colour according
to this, is entirely independent of and separate from light. It is
colour and not light which makes an impression upon a plate.
Might I humbly submit that if *all* things emit this force, and if this
force affects *all* plates "to a greater or less degree," how is a
gelatino-bromide plate ever to be manufactured or, above all,
stored? It is a waste of energy, however, to argue seriously against
such assertions.

Mr. Warner gives us some other interesting particulars about
"Od." He is gallant, and gives the fairer sex credit for possessing a
large share of the commodity. Flowers possess it also. They give
out light through it. Everything else affected gives out colour in
contradistinction to light. But it is just these little irregularities
which give the charm to the whole dissertation. When Mr.
Warner asserts, however, that it is clear that flowers emit light
through "Od" from the presence of a smell (flippancy again
suggests odour) he really transcends himself. The statement is so
gloriously and symmetrically absurd that it appears absolutely
brutal to suggest such botanical considerations as volatile oils, &c.,
especially in the face of the chirpy self-content with which Mr.
Warner remarks in the next line that "these things are easy of
proof, as must be apparent to any well-ordered mind." Alas! for
my poor cerebrum!

Let us take another delicious specimen of this gentleman's
method of reasoning. Here are two of the crisp statements in
which he indulges:- (1) Cleanliness induces to an abundance of

"Od." (2) People who have this force are especially fond of the colour blue. Now if we put the "Od" out of both questions, as being a common factor in the equation, we have it put seriously forward that clean people are especially fond of the colour blue – and this not as a mere playful hypothesis, but with the utmost confidence and dogmatism. I can only say that I have seen a procession of a certain well-known temperance organisation which would throw doubt upon the assertion.

I can hardly do justice to Mr. Warner's originality and daring in this hastily-written critique. Let me cull a few choice specimens of the flowers of science which lie scattered over the remainder of his communication. "The right side of every person is warmer than the left." *It isn't*; but no matter. "Odic impressions are either disagreeably warm or agreeably cool." There is something disagreeably cool in Mr. Warner's method of laying down the law. The gentleman gives us an experiment within the reach of all, which puts the existence of this galvanico-electro-hysterico-magnetic power beyond all cavil or argument. "If you hold up your leg," he says in his guileless way, "you find your foot grow cold. This is due to 'Od.' " If we had not been told we might have attributed it to the action of gravity upon the circulation of the blood. It is well to get at facts. Mr. Warner has another splendid illustration of the strange latent powers of "Od." It causes uneasiness and aversion at meeting some people, while others you may meet with indifference or pleasure. I have no doubt that if the gentleman observed a dialogue between the tax-gatherer and myself he would be surprised at the amount of "Od" which would be evolved. The last paragraph of Mr. Warner's letter I deprecate entirely as being out of place and in bad taste.

In conclusion: let me say that I know nothing of Mr. Warner, and that I should be most grieved to hurt his feelings in any way. Every man has a right to have his hobby, and to ride it, too, as long as he does not ride anyone down with it. When, however, a communication which abounds in scientific errors appears in an eminent scientific journal, it is not right that it should be allowed to pass uncorrected or unchallenged. Let Mr. Warner mature his views for another twelve years or so, and then give them light more logically and less dogmatically, while producing some show of reason for the faith that is in him.

A. CONAN DOYLE, M.B.

GENTLEMEN, – The following statement appears in Mr. W. Harding Warner's communication in last week's Journal:- "From our earth radiates an atmosphere called by men of science a 'photosphere,' or luminous halo. From this photosphere is thrown off another called a 'chromosphere,'" &c.

I have always understood that "men of science" applied the terms "photosphere" and "chromosphere" to the *sun*. The fact that these terms have been applied to the earth is new to me and may be to your readers generally, and for that reason I think it would be desirable if Mr. Warner would give the authority on which the statement is made. – I am, yours, &c.,

A. BROTHERS.

Manchester, July 17, 1883.

GENTLEMEN, – I beg to tender my thanks to Mr. A. Brothers for calling my attention in this week's Journal to an error in my article on the above. Instead of "From our earth radiates an atmosphere," it should have been "From the *sun* radiates an atmosphere called by men of science," &c., &c. The error arose in the hurry of copying from the note-book, and was not observed in the correction of the proof.

With regard to Mr. A. Conan Doyle's criticism upon the article: it is very plain to those few who understand about the new psychic force, "Od," that there are some men of science who know little or nothing of the laws of nature, and when something is stated that is beyond their powers of comprehension they turn it into ridicule, and thus expose themselves as to their want of knowledge in occult science. Excellent and jolly fellows they are, too, many of them, but they fail in this one point.

Let me assure Mr. Doyle that my feelings after reading his very laughable critique by the light of fact, as expressed by the pen of Baron von Reichenbach – from whose writings the ideas expressed were culled, and which have formed the subject of many experiments in the obtaining of photographs in the colours of nature and other purposes – that they are "*quite serene*;" as also upon the note by the Editors upon the photograph I sent of plants in a conservatory, of which quite twenty persons have seen the colour of the silver-leaf geraniums; so that we do not all see alike, and some of those here who examined the print are Londoners. – I am, yours, &c.

W. HARDING WARNER.

The Hollies, Clifton, July 21, 1883.

THE VOYAGE TO WEST AFRICA

———————◆◆◆———————

It had always been my intention to take a voyage as ship's surgeon when I had taken my degree, as I could in this way see something of the world, and at the same time earn a little of the money which I so badly needed if I were ever to start in practice for myself. When a man is in the very early twenties he will not be taken seriously as a practitioner, and though I looked old for my age, it was clear that I had to fill in my time in some other way. My plans were all exceedingly fluid, and I was ready to join the Army, Navy, Indian Service or anything which offered an opening. I had no reason to think that I would find a billet upon a passenger ship and had nearly forgotten that I had my name down, when I suddenly received a telegram telling me to come to Liverpool and to take medical charge of the African Steam Navigation Company's *Mayumba*, bound for the West Coast. In a week I was there, and on October 22, 1881, we started on our voyage.

The *Mayumba* was a trim little steamer of about 4,000 tons – a giant after my experience in the 200-ton whaler. She was built for commerce, carrying mixed cargoes to the coast and coming back with palm oil in puncheons, palm nuts in bulk, ivory and other tropical products. What with whale oil and palm oil there certainly seemed to be something greasy about my horoscope. There was room for twenty or thirty passengers, and it was for their behoof that I was paid some £12 a month.

It was well that we were seaworthy, for we put out in a violent gale, which became so bad as we emerged from the Mersey that

This descriptive account of Conan Doyle's experiences on the *Mayumba* between October 1881 and January 1882 forms the fifth chapter of his autobiography, *Memories and Adventures* (1924). It was first published in the *Strand Magazine* for November 1923, and acquires a new interest when set against his early articles which deal with the same subject.

we were forced into Holyhead for the night. Next day, in vile and thick weather, with a strong sea running, we made our way down the Irish Sea. I shall always believe that I may have saved the ship from disaster, for as I was standing near the officer of the watch I suddenly caught sight of a lighthouse standing out in a rift in the fog. It was on the port side and I could not imagine how any lighthouse could be on the port side of a ship which was, as I knew, well down on the Irish coast. I hate to be an alarmist, so I simply touched the mate's sleeve, pointed to the dim outline of the lighthouse, and said: 'Is that all right?" He fairly jumped as his eye lit upon it and he gave a yell to the men at the wheel and rang a violent signal to the engine-room. The lighthouse, if I remember right, was the Tuskar, and we were heading right into a rocky promontory which was concealed by the rain and fog.

I have been lucky in my captains, for Captain Gordon Wallace was one of the best, and we have kept in touch during the later years. Our passengers were mostly for Madeira, but there were some pleasant ladies bound for the Coast, and some unpleasant negro traders whose manners and bearing were objectionable, but who were patrons of the line and must, therefore, be tolerated. Some of these palm oil chiefs and traders have incomes of many thousands a year, but as they have no cultivated tastes they can only spend their money on drink, debauchery and senseless extravagance. One of them, I remember, had a choice selection of the demi-monde of Liverpool to see him off.

The storms followed us all the way down the Channel and across the Bay, which is normal, I suppose, at such a time of year. Everyone was seasick, so as doctor I had some work to do. However, before we reached Madeira we ran into fine weather and all our troubles were soon forgotten. One never realizes the comfort of a dry deck until one has been ankle-deep for a week. I missed the sea-boots and rough-and-ready dress of the whaler, for when one is in blue serge and gilt buttons one does not care to take a ducking. Just as we thought, however, that we were all right a worse gale than ever broke over us, the wind luckily being behind us, so that it helped us on our way. With jib, trysail and main staysail, which was as much as we could stand, we lurched and staggered, swept every now and then by the big Atlantic combers, which were phosphorescent at night, so that flames of liquid fire came coursing down the decks. Very glad we were when after a week of storm we saw the rugged peaks of Porto Sancto, an outlier of Madeira, and finally came to anchor in Funchal Bay. It was dark when we reached our moorings and it was good to see the lights of the town, and the great dark loom of the hills behind it. A lunar rainbow spanned the whole scene, a rare phenomenon which I have never seen before or since.

Teneriffe was our next stopping-place, Santa Cruz being the port of call. In those days it did a great trade in cochineal, which was derived from an insect cultivated on the cacti. When dried they furnished the dye, and a packet of the creatures averaged £350 at that time, but now I suppose that the German aniline dyes have killed the trade as completely as whaling has been killed by the mineral. A day later we were at Las Palmas, capital of Grand Canary, whence, looking back, we had a fine view of the famous Teneriffe Peak some 60 miles away. Leaving Las Palmas we were in the delightful region of the north-east trade-winds, the most glorious part of the ocean, seldom rough, yet always lively, with foam-capped seas and a clear sky. Day by day it grew hotter, however, and when we lost the Trades, and sighted the Isle de Los off the Sierra Leone coast, I began to realise what the Tropics meant. When you feel your napkin at meals to be an intolerable thing, and when you find that it leaves a wet weal across your white duck trousers, then you know that you really have arrived.

On November 9 we reached Freetown, the capital of Sierra Leone, our first port of call upon the African Main – a lovely spot but a place of death. Here our ladies left us, and indeed it was sad to see them go, for female lives are even shorter than male upon the coast. I speak of the days of malaria and blackwater fever, before Ronald Ross and others had done their great work of healing and prevention. It was a truly dreadful place in the early eighties, and the despair which reigned in the hearts of the white people made them take liberties with alcohol which they would not have dared to take in a healthier place. A year's residence seemed to be about the limit of human endurance. I remember meeting one healthy-looking resident who told me that he had been there three years. When I·congratulated him he shook his head. "I am a doomed man. I have advanced Bright's disease," said he. One wondered whether the colonies were really worth the price we had to pay.

From Sierra Leone we steamed to Monrovia, which is the capital of the negro republic of Liberia, which, as the name implies, was founded mainly by escaped slaves. So far as I could see it was orderly enough, though all small communities which take themselves seriously have a comic aspect. Thus at the time of the Franco-German War, Liberia is said to have sent out its single Customs boat, which represented its official Navy, and stopped the British mail-ship in order to send word to Europe that it did not intend to interfere in the matter.

It is a very monotonous view, for whether it is the Ivory Coast or the Gold Coast, or the Liberian shore, it always presents the same features – burning sunshine, a long swell breaking into a white line of surf, a margin of golden sand, and then the low green bush, with an occasional palm tree rising above it. If you have seen a mile, you have seen a thousand. As I write now, these ports at which we stopped, Grand Bassam, Cape Palmas, Accra, Cape Coast Castle, all form the same picture in my mind. One incident only I can remember. At some small village, the name of which I have forgotten, there came off a tall young Welshman in a state of furious excitement; his niggers had mutinied and he was in fear of his life. "There they are waiting for me!" he cried, and pointed to a dusky group upon the distant beach. We offered to take him on, but he could not leave his property, so all we could do was to promise to send a gunboat up from Cape Coast Castle. I have often wondered how such people got on after the German menace compelled us to draw in all our outlying fleets.

This coast is dotted at night with native fires, some of them of great extent, arising no doubt from their habit of burning the grass. It is interesting that in Hanno's account of his journey down the coast – the only piece of Carthaginian literature which has reached us – he talks also of the fires which he saw at night. As he speaks of gorillas it is probable that he got as far as the Gaboon, or south of the Line. He saw great volcanic activity, and the remains of it is still visible at Fernando Po, which is almost all volcanic. In Hanno's time, however, the hills were actually spouting fire and the country was a sea of flame, so that he dare not set foot on shore. I have wondered sometimes whether the last cataclysm at Atlantis may not have been much later than we think. The account of Plato puts it at about 9000 B.C., but it may well have been a gradual thing and the last spasm have been that of which Hanno saw the traces. All this activity which he described is exactly opposite the spot where the old continent was supposed to have been.

Our ships have rough-and-ready ways as they jog down the coast. Once we moved on while a hundred native visitors were still on board. It was funny to see them dive off and make for their canoes. One of them had a tall hat, an umbrella, and a large coloured picture of the Saviour – all of which he had bought at the trading booths which the men rig up in the forecastle. These impedimenta did not prevent him from swimming to his boat. At another minor port, since we were pressed for time, we simply threw our consignment of barrel staves overboard, knowing that soon or late they would wash up on the beach, though how the real owner could make good his claim to them I do not know. Occasionally the native scores in this game. Some years ago, before Dahomey was annexed by the French, the captain took the oil casks on board at Whydah by means of a long rope and a donkey engine, an ingenious way of avoiding the surf, which came to a sudden stop when a company of the famous Amazons appeared and threatened to fire upon the ship if they did not pay their dues to the surf boats in the ordinary fashion.

I had myself to pay my dues to the climate, for on November 18 I find an eloquent gap in my diary. We had reached Lagos, and there, rolling in a greasy swell off that huge lagoon, the germ or the mosquito or whatever it was reached me and I was down with a very sharp fever. I remember staggering to my bunk and then all was blotted out. As I was myself doctor there was no one to look after me and I lay for several days fighting it out with Death in a very small ring and without a second. It speaks well for my constitution that I came out a victor. I remember no psychic experience, no vision, no fears, nothing save a nightmare fog from which I emerged as weak as a child. It must have been a close call, and I had scarcely sat up before I heard that another victim who got it at the same time was dead.

A week later found me, convalescent and full of energy once more, up the Bonny River, which certainly never got its name from the Scotch adjective, for it is in all ways hateful with its brown smelling stream and its mango swamps. The natives were all absolute savages, offering up human sacrifices to sharks and crocodiles. The captain had heard the screams of the victims and seen them dragged down to the water's edge, while on another occasion he had seen the protruding skull of a man who had been buried in an ant-heap. It is all very well to make game of the missionaries, but how could such people ever be improved if it were not for the labours of devoted men?

We called at Fernando Po, and later at Victoria, a lovely little settlement upon the Main, with the huge peak of the Cameroons rising behind it. A dear homely Scotch lassie was playing the part of missionary there, and if she did not evangelise she at least civilised, which is more important. It lies in a beautiful bay studded with islands and well wooded all round. For some reason the whole style of the scenery changes completely here, and it is the more welcome after the thousand miles of monotony to the north. All this land went, for some reason, to Germany later, and has now reverted to the French, who are not, as a rule, good Colonial neighbours. I went ashore at Victoria, and I cannot forget my thrill when what I thought was a good-sized blue bird passed me and I found that it was a butterfly.

To reach Old Calabar we had to steam for 60 miles up the Old Calabar River, the channel lying so near the shore that we brushed the trees on one side. I lay in wait with my rifle, but though I saw the swirl of several alligators none emerged. Old Calabar seemed the largest and most prosperous place we had visited, but here also the hand of death was over all, and it was "eat, drink, and be merry" for the old and unsatisfactory reason. Here again we met one of these young lady pioneers of civilisation. Civilisation is the better, but it is a stern and dreadful call which summons a woman to such a work.

Getting a canoe, I ascended the river for several miles to a place called Creektown. Dark and terrible mangrove swamps lay on either side with gloomy shades where nothing that is not horrible could exist. It is indeed a foul place. Once in an isolated tree, standing in a flood, I saw an evil-looking snake, worm-coloured and about 3 feet long. I shot him and saw him drift down stream. I learned later in life to give up killing animals, but I confess that I have no particular compunctions about that one. Creektown is in native territory, and the King sent down a peremptory order that we should report ourselves to him, but as it sounded ominous and might mean a long delay we got our paddles out and were soon back in British waters.

I had a curious experience one morning. A large ribbon-shaped fish, about 3 or 4 feet long, came up and swam upon the surface near the ship. Having my gun handy, I shot it. I don't think five seconds could have elapsed before another larger and thicker fish – a big catfish, I should say – darted up from the depths, seized the wounded fish by the middle, and dragged it down. So murderous is the food-search, and so keen the watch in Nature! I saw something similar in the mixed tank of an aquarium once, where a fish stunned himself by swimming against the glass front, and was instantly seized and devoured by his neighbour. A strange fish to which I was introduced at Calabar was the electrical torpedo fish. It is handed to you in an earthenware saucer – a quiet little drab creature about 5 inches long – and you are asked to tickle its back. Then you learn exactly how high you can jump.

The death-like impression of Africa grew upon me. One felt that the white man with his present diet and habits was an intruder who was never meant to be there, and that the great sullen brown continent killed him as one crushes nits. I find in my diary:

"Oh Africa, where are the charms
   That sages have seen in thy face?
Better dwell in Old England on alms
   Than be rich in that terrible place."

The life aboard ship, however, was an easy and, in some ways, a luxurious one – too luxurious for a young man who had his way to make in the world. Premature comfort is a deadly enervating thing. I remember considering my own future – I stood upon the poop with a raging thunderstorm around me – and seeing very clearly that one or two more such voyages would sap my simple habits and make me unfit for the hard struggle which any sort of success would need. The idea of success in literature had never crossed my mind. It was still of medicine only that I thought, but I knew by my Birmingham experience how long and rough a path it was for those who had no influence and could not afford to buy. Then and there was surely one of the turning-points of my life. A "Wander-Jahr" is good, but two "Wander-Jahre" may mean damnation – and it is hard to stop. I find that on the same day of fruitful meditation I swore off alcohol for the rest of the voyage. I drank quite freely at this period of my life, having a head and a constitution which made me fairly immune, but my reason told me that the unbounded cocktails of West Africa were a danger, and with an effort I cut them out. There is a certain subtle pleasure in abstinence, and it is only socially that it is difficult. If we were all abstainers as a matter of course, like the real Mahomedans, none of us would ever miss it.

I did a mad thing at Cape Coast Castle, for, in a spirit either of bravado or pure folly, I swam round the ship – or at least for some length along her and back again. I suppose it was the consideration that black folk go freely into the water which induced me to do it. For some reason white folk do not share the same immunity. As I was drying myself on deck I saw the triangular back fin of a shark rise to the surface. Several times in my life I have done utterly reckless things with so little motive that I have found it difficult to explain them to myself afterwards. This was one of them.

The most intelligent and well-read man whom I met on the Coast was a negro, the American Consul at Monrovia.* He came on with us as a passenger. My starved literary side was eager for good talk, and it was wonderful to sit on deck discussing Bancroft and Motley, and then suddenly realise that you were talking to one who had possibly been a slave himself, and was certainly the son of slaves. He had thought a good deal about African travel.

* Henry Highland Garnet (1815–1882)

"The only way to explore Africa is to go without arms and with few servants. You would not like it in England if a body of men came armed to the teeth and marched through your land. The Africans are quite sensitive." It was the method of Livingstone as against the method of Stanley. The former takes the braver and better man.

This negro gentleman did me good, for a man's brain is an organ for the formation of his own thoughts and also for the digestion of other people's and it needs fresh fodder. We had, of course, books aboard the ship, but neither many nor good. I cannot trace that I made any mental or spiritual advancement during the voyage, but I added one more experience to my chaplet, and I suppose it all goes to some ultimate result in character or personality. I was a strong full-blooded young man, full of the joy of life, with nothing of what Oliver Wendell Holmes calls "pathological piety and tuberculous virtues." I was a man among men. I walked ever among pitfalls and I thank all ministering angels that I came through, while I have a softened heart for those who did not.

Our voyage home – oil-gathering from port to port on the same but reversed route – was uneventful until the very last stride, when just as we were past Madeira the ship took fire. Whether it was the combustion of coal dust has never been determined, but certainly the fire broke out in the bunkers, and as there was only a wooden partition between these bunkers and a cargo of oil, we were in deadly danger. For the first day we took it lightly, as a mere smoulder, and for a second and third day we were content to seal the gratings as far as possible, to play down on it with the hose, and to shift the coal away from the oil. On the fourth morning, however, things took a sudden turn for the worse. I copy from my log book:

"January 9. I was awakened early in the morning by the purser, Tom King, poking his head in at my door and informing me that the ship was in a blaze, and that all hands had been called and were working down below. I got my clothes on, but when I came on deck nothing was to be seen of it save thick volumes of smoke from the bunker ventilators, and a lurid glow down below. I offered to go down, but there seemed to be as many working as could be fitted in. I was then asked to call the passengers. I waked each in turn, and they all faced the situation very bravely and coolly. One, a Swiss, sat up in his bunk, rubbed his eyes, and in answer to my remark: 'The ship is on fire!' said: I have often been on ships that were on fire.' 'Splendide mendax' – but a good spirit! All day we fought the flames, and the iron side of the ship was red-hot at one point. Boats were prepared and provisioned and no doubt at the worst we could row or sail them to Lisbon, where my dear sisters would be considerably surprised if their big brother walked in. However, we are getting the better of it, and by evening those ominous pillars of smoke were down to mere wisps. So ends an ugly business!"

On January 14 we were in Liverpool once more, and West Africa was but one more of the cinema reels of memory. It is, I am told, very much improved now in all things. My old friend and cricket companion, Sir Fred. Guggisberg, is Governor at Accra and has asked me to see the old ground under very different auspices. I wish I could, but the sands still run and there is much to be done.

NOTES

———————◆———————

AFTER CORMORANTS WITH A CAMERA

The Isle of May lies at the mouth of the Firth of Forth about six miles from Anstruther and the neighbouring burgh of Crail. It was a popular destination for tourists from Edinburgh who could go the whole way by boat or take the train up the coast and then cross to the island. Doyle could have made the journey on any number of occasions, but it is likely that the visit took place in July or August 1881.

Although the companions may refer to real people, and one can speculate on the author's friends who might have taken part like Bryan Charles Waller who was a close family friend, or James Ryan who was Doyle's contemporary at Stonyhurst and Edinburgh and whose mother was close to Mary Doyle, it seems more likely that the author's imagination was allowed a free rein. The "Doctor" could well be a self-portrait as the puns and abstruse riddles are apparent in the text, while the narrator, "Bob", is presented with no individuality.

More interest is likely to be attached to the names of the companions who did not take part. The use of "Holmes" precedes Sherlock Holmes by five years and was probably based on Oliver Wendell Holmes, though there were a number of students with that name at Edinburgh University such as David Holmes who became an M.B. in 1877, or James Holmes who became an M.D. in the same year. The same is true of "Godfrey" as there was a student with this name a year senior and another a year junior to Doyle. For Sherlockian scholars there are other points of interest. Singleton (perhaps after Defoe's *Captain Singleton*) brings to mind the unrecorded case of the Conk-Singleton forgery, Anstruther was the name of the doctor who stood in for Watson when he was called away to Boscombe Valley, and the subject matter and title of the article suggest a case mentioned in "The Adventure of the Veiled Lodger", the story concerning the politician, the light-house and the trained cormorant. One could even claim that the article represents Doyle's first detective story, as the camera serves as a means of collecting evidence of a crime. Jack Hawkins is interesting for a different reason, as this was the name of his first resident patient, who died on the premises and whose sister became Doyle's wife. This is coincidental as Doyle did not meet Jack Hawkins until March 1885 (though there might have been a previous encounter in a railway carriage as described in Doyle's semi-autobiographical novel about the period, *The Stark Munro Letters*).

The impressive use of Scottish terms owed much to Doyle's experience as an assistant to Dr. Joseph Bell. "When I took over his outpatient work he warned me that a knowledge of Scottish idioms was necessary and I, with the confidence of youth, declared that I had got it. The sequel was amusing. On one of the first days an old man came who, in response to my question, declared that he had a 'bealin in his oxter'. This fairly beat me, much to Bell's amusement. It turned out that the words meant an abcess in the armpit" (*Memories and Adventures*, p.26).

Doyle used the Isle of May as the setting for the death of Cowles in "John Barrington Cowles. The Story of a Medical Student", which was first published in *Cassell's Saturday Journal* in April 1884. The narrator, Robert Armitage, or "Bob" as in the article, describes how he travelled with Cowles through the highlands of Scotland and afterwards down the east coast: "In one of these peregrinations of ours we visited the Isle of May, an island near the mouth of the Firth of Forth, which, except in the tourist season, is singularly barren and desolate. Beyond the keeper of the lighthouse there are only one or two families of poor fisher-folk, who sustain a precarious existence by their nets, and by the capture of cormorants and Solan geese." The two men engage rooms in one of the fishermen's huts, but a few days later Cowles rushes out into the night and meets his death falling from the cliffs.

1 "a most ancient and fishlike smell"] *The Tempest*, II. ii: 'A very ancient and fishlike smell'.
3 the recommendation which appeared in THE BRITISH JOURNAL OF PHOTOGRAPHY] 3 June 1881, p.227: "Tin trays or dishes are very useful for alkaline pyro. or ferrous oxalate development . . . The trays are very light, cost a mere trifle, can be obtained at any ironmonger's establishment and made any size to order."
3 the boiling method of our worthy chief editor] W.B. Bolton first suggested boiling, as a way of shortening the time needed to

gain sensitiveness, in 1879. His process is described at length in the *British Journal Photographic Almanac* for 1881, "The Boiling Method of Emulsification in Theory and Practice", pp.25-34. The almanac is mentioned in Doyle's article and would have been his source.

5 to quote Mark Twain, is "not quite as straight as a rainbow nor as crooked as a corkscrew"] *The Innocents Abroad*, Chapter 44 (*The New Pilgrim's Progress*, Chapter 13): "The street called Straight is straighter than a corkscrew, but not as straight as a rainbow."

5 "Dinna forget"]   A Scottish ballad with words by John Imlah and music by V.P. Millard, published in 1831. It is a lament by a girl at being parted from her lover, hence the "delicate allusion":

> "Dinna forget! laddie, dinna forget!
> Ne'er make me rue that we ever have met;
> Wide tho' we sever, parted for ever,
> Willie! when far a wa, dinna forget!"
>
> *&c.*

5 "was na' fou, he was na' fou"] Possibly a reference to a poem by Robert Burns. "Death and Dr. Hornbrook": "I wasna fou, but just had plenty!" Or "Willie Brewed a Peck o' Maut": "We are na fou, we're nae that fou, / But just a drappie in our ee."

5 "double ten" by Greener] W.W. Greener was one of the foremost British gunmakers and an authority on firearms. His book, *The Gun and Its Development*, was published in 1881. The term "Greener" became synonymous with a type of shotgun irrespective of the maker in the same way as the "Winchester".

9 "The Midshipmite"] A song with words by Fred E. Weatherly and music by Stephen Adams, published in 1879. It is a tale of the Crimean War in which a young midshipman who has volunteered to spike the "Rooshan" guns is wounded and then brought back to the ship.

ON THE SLAVE COAST WITH A CAMERA

Doyle applied for the post of surgeon aboard the S.S. *Mayumba* while he was acting as an assistant to Dr. Reginald Ratcliffe Hoare in Birmingham. On Saturday 22 October 1881 the ship sailed from the Coburg Docks in Liverpool on the regular run for the West Coast of Africa.

The ship, an iron screw barque, had been built by Edward J. Harland of Queen's Island, Belfast, in 1859, and was of 1492 gross tons (Doyle described it incorrectly in his autobiography as being 4000 tons). Originally named the *Sicilian*, it was built for Bibby and Company. New engines and boilers were installed in 1872 and it was acquired the following year by Fred Leyland and Company from whom the African Steamships Company chartered it in 1880 with an option to buy. It was then renamed the *Mayumba*. A. Sinclair of 20 Water Street, Liverpool, acted as the consignee for the ship which carried merchandise, salt, and mail, as well as a number of passengers, and which was commanded by Captain H.G. Wallace.

On 29 October the ship docked at Madeira, then after putting in at Teneriffe and Grand Canary, it continued round the coast as far as Old Calabar. Here it turned and sailed for home, calling again at the various ports visited on the outward journey: Fernando Po, Bonny, Lagos, Quittah, Addah, Accra, Winnebah, Cape Coast Castle, Salt Pond, Elmina, Half Jack, Grand Lahon, Cape Palmas, Grand Bassa, Sierra Leone, Ile de Los, Grand Canary, Teneriffe, and Madeira. The ship reached Liverpool on 14 January 1882 and berthed in the Morpeth Dock. Its cargo on the homeward journey consisted of casks of palm oil, barrels of black oil, bags of palm kernels, bales of cotton, benniseed, ivory, and other goods, as well as the mails and passengers. The latter, restricted on the final leg to those with cabins, had been swelled while near the coast by large numbers of deck passengers travelling between the ports.

The *Mayumba* had been involved in a collision in 1881 when it sank the barque *Severn* off Madeira. On Doyle's voyage it narrowly escaped disaster on the way out, and when it left Madeira on 6 January 1882 a fire broke out aboard. This appears to have caused some damage and the vessel was sold that year to C.R. Gilchrist of Chapel Street, Liverpool. It was finally scuttled in 1884 when another fire broke out while it was at Arzue in Algeria.

The three articles which Doyle wrote for the *British Journal of Photography* about his experiences on the *Mayumba* may be compared with the chapter of his autobiography which was first published in the *Strand Magazine* for November 1923. The later piece (reprinted as an appendix in this volume), like the earlier ones, was based on the log which he had kept at the time. Each complements the other but the one conspicuous difference is that photography is not mentioned in the autobiography.

Doyle's impression of West Africa was one of heat, monotony, and unpleasantness. After his return he told his mother that he had no intention of going back to Africa: "The pay is less than I could make by my pen in the same time, and the climate is atrocious." A more forthright condemnation is found in a letter he wrote to Mrs. Charlotte Thwaites Drummond from Bonny on 22 November 1881: "Never was there such a hole of a place, it is good for nothing but swearing at. I am just recovering from a smart attack of fever, and am so weak that the pen feels like an oar though I was only on my back for three days. It is our summer here, and while you are having crisp frosty mornings (it makes my feet tingle to think of them) we have an apoplectic looking sun glaring down at us in a disgusting manner, while there is never a breath of air, save when a whiff of miasma is borne off the land. Here we are steaming from one dirty little port to another dirty little port, all as like as two peas, and only to be distinguished by comparing the smell of the inhabitants, though they all smell as if they had become prematurely putrid and should be buried without unnecessary delay. We have come 2000 miles down the coast now, and a hundred yards might stand for the lot – a row of breakers – a yellow strip of sand and a line of palm trees . . ." Although his fever had been severe, he was anxious to keep it from his mother: "I don't want her to see a grumbling letter, else she would begin hunting up a coffin for me and writing obituary notices" (a.l.s., 23 November 1881).

The journey did provide many colourful details for Doyle's stories. There are many references, for example, in *The Firm of Girdlestone*, or there is the "elegant rendering" in verse of a shipping company's instructions to one of their captains which appears in "Cyprian Overbeck Wells" (1886):

"From England, Captain, you must steer a
Course directly to Madeira,
Land the casks of salted beef,
Then away to Teneriffe.
Pray be careful, cool, and wary
With the merchants of Canary.
When you leave them make the most
Of the trade winds to the coast.
Down it you shall sail as far
As the land of Calabar,
And from there you'll onward go
To Bonny and Fernando Po – "

Two books which he had taken with him are mentioned in "Before My Bookcase", a series of six articles written for *Great*

Thoughts in 1894 which later formed the basis of *Through the Magic Door*. The one book from which he had derived most profit and pleasure was, he says, his copy of Macaulay's *Essays*: "This one has been with me on the sweltering Gold Coast, and formed part of my scanty kit when I went a-whaling in the Arctic" (*Great Thoughts*, 5 May 1894). Another book which he describes is his copy of Kammario's *L'Atmosphere*, "a very gorgeous one it is, with its coloured illustrations and its red and gold cover. The book has a small history and I value it. A young Frenchman dying of fever upon the West Coast of Africa gave it to me as a professional fee. The sight of it takes me back to a little ship's bunk and a sallow face with large black eyes looking out at me" (*Great Thoughts*, 30 June 1894).

Although Doyle did not give a talk about West Africa to the Portsmouth Literary and Scientific Society, as he was to do with his Arctic Voyage, he did mention it on a number of occasions. He told an amusing story after a meeting on 3 December 1889 at which his friend, Major General A.W. Drayson, had spoken on "The Art of Killing". The *Hampshire Telegraph* (7 December 1889) reports: "Dr. Conan Doyle (Hon. Sec.) amusingly detailed how, when he voyaged to the West Coast of Africa as a ship's surgeon, he innocently took out quite a battery of Birmingham guns and ammunition, expecting the negroes to gladly buy them with gold. He took the weapons up and down the coast, but found that the chiefs, who allowed nobody but themselves to acquire firearms, were already armed with Remington rifles, Winchester repeaters and other modern makes which he himself had never seen. Eventually he did succeed in bartering one of the weapons for a tooth-brush." Two years before, he had joined in the discussion which followed Dr. G.H. Smith's paper on "Three years residence in the Congo": "Dr. Conan Doyle described a visit he had paid to the West Coast of Africa, and spoke of the natives as of the most degraded. He asked if it were probable that Government of the State would be permanent?" (*Hampshire Post*, 9 December 1887). The meeting has an added significance as Doyle took up the cause of Congo reform in 1909, when, with the help of E.D. Morel, he collected details of the Belgian misrule and wrote *The Crime of the Congo*. This was to bring him into contact with Mark Twain, whose works had been a strong influence on his early articles. Both were indignant about the situation in the Congo and both wrote about it. Doyle mentions Twain's book in the preface to the American edition of *The Crime of the Congo* where he refers to the "incorruptible evidence of the kodak": "Any American citizen who will glance at Mark Twain's 'King Leopold's Soliloquy' will see some samples of that." He sent a copy to Twain, who was by then a sick and dying man with only a few months to live, and received an answer from Albert Bigelow Paine on 29 October 1909: "Mr. Clemens, who is not very robust these days, has asked me to reply to you concerning the Congo matter. He is deeply interested in the subject; so deeply, in fact, that any intimate consideration of it excites and distresses him to a degree which we think dangerous. He therefore does not permit himself to read any matter pertaining to the cruelties practised there, or to write anything further on the subject." Paine went on to thank Doyle, on Twain's behalf, for the booklet and for his cordial letter.

When Doyle went to Africa in 1881 and if he indeed took a camera, the last thing he would have expected was to gain psychic results. Forty years later just such a result was obtained and the photograph was one which he rated highly. It is described in *The Case for Spirit Photography* (p.31): "I have, as an example, a photograph before me as I write which was taken by Mr. Boyd, the respected provost of a Scotch Borough, upon a recent journey which he made to the West Coast of Africa. On taking a small group of natives he found an extra of a woman and child (negroes) upon his plate. This extra figure is surrounded and surmounted by the psychic arch in an exaggerated form."

Doyle went to South Africa at the time of the Boer War and made a final trip in 1928 when he lectured on spiritualism. On his last trip he was again buffeted by severe storms in the Bay of Biscay and the ship, the *Windsor Castle*, put in at both Madeira and the Canary Islands, but it did not stop on the coast. Doyle's description of the journey which he jotted down at the time, and which forms the first chapters of *Our African Winter*, includes no mention of his first voyage.

THE SLAVE COAST] The Slave Coast runs from the River Volta to the Calabar River.
13 *Punch's* time-honoured advice before matrimony – "Don't."] *Punch*, 1845, Vol.8, p.1: "Advice to persons about to marry. – Don't."
14 the precedent of Colonel Stuart Wortley] Colonel Stuart Wortley (1832-90) was an important photographer of the period and was closely involved in the running of many of the British photographic societies. He had already visited India, but for reasons of health embarked on a world tour in December 1879, going to Australia, Tahiti, and the South Sea Islands, and returning through the United States. He hired a yacht in Tahiti and

the marine photographs he took here and elsewhere were considered exceptional.

15 "go down to the sea in ships"] Psalm 107, l.23: "Some went down to the sea in ships, doing business on the great waters." *The Firm of Girdlestone*, 4: "You remember what is said about those who go down to the sea in ships. They see the wonders of the deep, and in return they incur some little danger."

15 paraphrasing Tom Moore – "You may scowl at the surgeon, and swear if you will, but the smell of his hartshorn will hang round you still"] Thomas Moore, *Irish Melodies*, "Farewell! – But Whenever You Welcome the Hour", ls.23-4: "You may break, you may shatter the vase, if you will, / But the scent of the roses will hang round it still."

16 "astonish the natives"] As Godfrey C. Mundy, *Our Antipodes: or residence and rambles in the Australasian colonies*, 1857, 104: "The brutal drunkenness and reckless debauchery of the Pakehas actually 'astonished the natives'."

16 the ill-fated "Clan Macduff"] The *Clan Macduff*, formerly the *City of Oxford*, sailed from Liverpool on 18 October 1881 bound for Bombay. The bilge pumps became blocked on 19 October and a steam pipe was washed away. The ship began sinking on the following day and went down during the night of 22 October.

17 Nelson the only defeat he ever sustained] The unsuccessful attack on Santa Cruz de Teneriffe on 24 July 1797 when Nelson was disabled by the loss of his arm.

18 "The March of the Camera Men"] "The March of the Cameron Men", a song with words and music by Mary M. Campbell, 1861.

18 "The White Man's Grave"] Sir W. Butler, *Autobiography*, 1873, 9: "What did it matter if the Gold Coast had been the White Man's Grave ever since Columbus had been there?"

18 the model colony of Liberia] This was founded by the American Colonisation Society in 1822, its capital, Monrovia, being named after the American president.

21 one of our crew succumbed] A description of a burial at sea is given in *The Firm of Girdlestone*, III: ". . . he's dead o' fever, poor dear, and lying in Bonny river wi' a cannon ball at his feet, as the carpenter himself told me who sewed him up."

22 "Better fifty years of Europe than a cycle of Cathay."] Tennyson, *Locksley Hall*, l.184.

UP AN AFRICAN RIVER WITH THE CAMERA

23   the good ship "Syria"] It is unclear why Doyle should have referred to the ship by this name rather than the *Mayumba*, which was the correct name and that used in the other two articles about his voyage.

24   "Lotus eaters" – "Our home / Lies far beyond the deep; we will no longer roam" –] Tennyson, "The Lotos-Eaters", 44–5: "Our Island home / Is far beyond the wave; we will no longer roam."

25   "happy and glorious"] Henry Carey, "God Save the King". The British national anthem.

25   "gird up my loins"]*Job*, xxxviii. 3: "Gird up now thy loins like a man."

25   *Scarabœus Camiferus*] Possibly afer Oliver Wendell Holmes' "scarabœus grammaticus" (*The Autocrat of the Breakfast Table*, V).

26   an enormously exaggerated worm livid in colour, with a couple of little beady eyes and a tongue that flickered venomously in front of him.] Doyle may have recalled this incident when writing "The Problem of Thor Bridge". Watson mentions the case of Isadora Persano, "who was found stark staring mad with a matchbox in front of him which contained a remarkable worm, said to be unknown to science".

27   Kroomen] A negro race on the coast of Liberia who were noted as seamen.

27   Mandingoes] The Mandinka traced their origins back to the great empire of ancient Mali. By 1881 they were becoming one of the foremost political units and would have been met with at Freetown.

27   Houssars] Hausas from the Hausa states.

27   Ashantees] Asante. The war of 1874 had destroyed their power. The tribe would have been encountered at Cape Coast Castle.

27   "linked sweetness long drawn out"] Milton, *L'Allegro*, 140.

29   "Britons never, never, never," &c] "Rule Britannia": "Britons never, never, never shall be slaves." [James Thompson, *Alfred: a Masque*, 1740: "Britons never will be slaves!"]

DRY PLATES ON A WET MOOR

This article is of special interest as it describes Dartmoor, used twenty years later as the setting for *The Hound of the Baskervilles*.

The journey from Plymouth to Tavistock with a stop-over at Roborough is described as having taken place in August 1882, though it may actually have been in late June or July. It followed the six extraordinary months which Doyle spent with Dr. George T. Budd in Plymouth.

Doyle had met George Budd, who was a year senior and already married, when they were medical students at Edinburgh. After the death of his father, William Budd, George had taken over the practice in Bristol – where Doyle visited him in the autumn of 1881 – but this venture was not a success. George therefore moved to Plymouth where his uncle, Dr. John Budd, had been well-known. Here he acquired premises at 1 Durnford Street and soon afterwards sent Doyle a telegram announcing that he had met with prodigious success and offering to take him as a partner with a salary of not less than £300 a year. By giving free consultations Budd was attracting a large number of patients and some of these he passed on to Doyle who was given a consulting room at Durnford Street and lodgings in the Budd's house at 6 Elliot Terrace.

The partnership was to be short-lived as letters from Doyle's mother, who disapproved of his association with the Budds, fell into their hands and caused a rift. It was decided that Doyle would be given a pound a week until he had set himself up in a practice of his own. He therefore set out for Tavistock. He later told Mrs. Drummond: "I first as you know went to Plymouth where Budd and I did not pull together very well. I then went prospecting to Tavistock in Devon but could not see anything to suit. I then set sail to Portsmouth, a town where I knew nobody, and nobody knew me (which was a point in my favour)." He had less than £10 in his pocket when he boarded the Irish steamer for Portsmouth, and soon after his arrival received a letter from Budd announcing that the pound a week was to be stopped.

Doyle had no further personal contact with Budd, who died in 1889 at the age of 34, leaving a widow and four children, but the experience was never forgotten, indeed it played an important part in the development of many of Doyle's fictional characters. The "Genius" in this article is probably based on Budd, who was also to appear very thinly disguised in a short story called "Crabbe's Practice" (1884) and in *The Stark Munro Letters* (1895). In the latter, Budd appears as Dr. Cullingworth (the name also used in Doyle's autobiography), while Doyle portrays himself with some artistic licence as Dr. Stark Munro. His visit to Tavistock, here called Stockwell, is described as follows: ". . . I started off for Stockwell, taking with me only a bag, for it was merely a prospecting expedition, and I intended to return for my luggage if I saw reason for hope. Alas! there was not the faintest . . . back I came, rather heavy at heart, and having spent ten or twelve shillings which I could ill afford." (*The Stark Munro Letters*, X).

While Doyle may have visited Roborough on an earlier occasion as it is only about five miles north of Plymouth, it seems more likely that he did stay at the Admiral Vernon on his way to Tavistock. The setting was used in "The Winning Shot", a short story he wrote soon afterwards which was published in *Bow Bells* during July 1883. It takes place at "Colonel Pillar's place at Roborough" in August 1882 and concerns the mysterious Octavius Gaster whose powers resemble those of Zamiel in *Der Freischutz*, for he makes the narrator's lover shoot himself when firing the winning shot. Certain extracts are worth quoting here as they contain close parallels with the article. The narrator, Charlotte Underwood, sits gazing out dreamily at "the great wilderness of Dartmoor, which stretched away to the horizon, ruddy and glowing in the light of the sinking sun, save where some rugged tor stood out in bold relief against the scarlet background". She walks out with Charley Pillar: "Not a living creature did we meet upon our solitary walk, save a few scraggy Devonshire sheep, who looked at us wistfully, and followed us for some distance, as if curious as to what could possibly have induced us to trespass upon their domain. It was almost dark before we reached the little stream, which comes gurgling down through a precipitous glen, and meanders away to help to form the Plymouth 'leat' . . . 'Strangers have been found dead on it before now,' continued Charley. 'They lose themselves, and then wander in a circle until they fall from fatigue.' "

The visit provided details for some of the Sherlock Holmes stories which precede *The Hound of the Baskervilles* – "The Adventure of Silver Blaze", for example, is set near Tavistock – but it was, without doubt, the memory of it which was in Doyle's mind when he met Bertram Fletcher Robinson (1872-1907), who was a

native of Ipplepen in Devon. The two men travelled back on the
same ship from South Africa and visited Cromer together in
March 1901 when the idea for *The Hound of the Baskervilles* was
born. At the end of that month they went to Devon and from
Rowe's Duchy Hotel in Princeton made exploratory expeditions
over the moors. "We did 14 miles over the moor today and we are
now pleasantly weary," he told his mother on 2 April 1901. "It is a
great place, very sad and wild, dotted with the dwellings of pre-
historic man, strange monoliths and huts and graves . . . you may
walk all day and never see a soul . . ."

31 a cross between Oscar Wilde and a gamekeeper] In 1882
Doyle took his girl friend, Elmore Welden, to see Gilbert and
Sullivan's comic opera *Patience*. This was probably his first introduction to the aesthetic movement. Two years later, in April
1884, he would have been able to hear Wilde lecture at the
Portland Hall, Southsea. In August 1889 he met Wilde when both
were invited to write for *Lippincott's Magazine*.
31 proverbial tombstone] "As silent as the grave", or as Lang-
land has it "As doumbe as deth".
33 the Eddystone Lighthouse] This was the fourth lighthouse at
Eddystone; designed by Sir James Douglas, it was completed in
1882.
36 Kingsley's *Westward Ho!* . . . Amyas Leigh rode across with his
shipmates from Plymouth to Bideford . . . the spot where Salvation Yeo slew the King of the Gubbins] Charles Kingsley,
Westward Ho! XIV. The Gubbins were a band of 16th-century
robbers who lived in caves and multiplied without marriage. The
spot where Salvation Yeo killed their king was at a wayside inn to
the north east of Brent Tor, about four miles north of Tavistock.
   Kingsley was a much greater influence on Doyle's own historical romances than he afterwards acknowledged. The title of the
chapter he refers to, "How Salvation Yeo Slew the King of the
Gubbins", is, for example, similar to those used for the Brigadier
Gerard stories, such as "How Brigadier Gerard Slew the Brothers
of Ajaccio"; but the influence extends beyond that to the style and
even to a certain "muscular Christianity" which creeps into novels
like *Sir Nigel*.

A FEW TECHNICAL HINTS

Emulsifying: This article was written in October 1882 and therefore preceded the meeting in November at which Burton announced his modified process. The original emulsion process to which Doyle refers is given in Burton's *ABC of Modern Photography* (1882) as follows: 400 grains of Nitrate of Silver with 8 fluid ounces of water, added to 220 grains of Bromide of Ammonium with 15 grains of Iodide of Ammonium, 15 grains of Chloride Ammonium, 80 grains of Gelatine and 8 fluid ounces of water, added to 450 grains of Autotype gelatine.

The ruby red colour of the emulsion appeared when the plate had been coated with the newly made emulsion. Burton states: "It will be seen that on looking at a light through the plate the light appears ruby red."

Boiling: The use of gelatine was first suggested in 1871, but it was not until 1878 that Charles Bennett discovered that gelatine emulsion gained in sensitiveness when heated and that the speed of the process could be increased by the addition of ammonia. The boiling process which followed from this was developed by W.B. Bolton in 1879 and described in the *British Journal Photographic Almanac* in 1881. The addition of iodide was suggested by Captain Abney in an article for the *British Journal of Photography* on 14 October 1881, "Iodide in Gelatine Emulsion" (pp.528-9) as this prevented halation and fogging, and gave an improved quality to the developed image.

Washing: This was an essential part of the process. The combination of bromide of ammonium and nitrate of silver produced the desired bromide of silver, but also gave nitrate of ammonium which damaged the emulsion if left in. As it was impossible to get exact quantities of the salts to allow for a perfect conversion without either an excess of nitrate of silver or bromide of potassium, it was necessary to use an excess of soluble bromide which could then be washed off. The gelatine solution was in the form of a jelly which was insoluble in cold water and could therefore be broken up and soaked. It was dried by being pushed through a "squeezer" or drained in a sieve.

Coating the Plates: The emulsion would be reheated and poured over the glass plate which was held in a "levelling shelf" so that it could be spread evenly with a glass rod.

Gelatine plates tended to "fog" in all but non-actinic light and this led to the creation of dark rooms in which the light was shaded either in orange or ruby glass. This prevented the "light fog". The red fog, which had become less common in 1882, plagued many earlier attempts. It appeared as a deep red stain on the surface of the film or as a faint stain, and was caused by the decomposition of the gelatine. The green fog was caused by a silver deposit and occurred in the alkaline pyrogallic developers when the plate was under-exposed and the development forced. The chemical fog was usually the result of an error in the preparation of the plate when the silver salt reduced the developer without the light having acted on it. It was caused by too great alkalinity.

Drying: The drying box was a ventilated container with racks into which the plates could be put. A number of these were designed either with their own heat source or able to stand on a stove.

Frilling: This was the name given to the swelling of the film at the edges and the consequent parting from the glass plate which resembled the frills on a lady's dress. It was also used to describe blisters which occurred in the centre of the plates. Mixing a little methylated spirit with the developer, as suggested by Doyle, was one method of preventing it, though this tended to delay the development. Another method was to use paraffin or any greasy substance to prevent the developer penetrating the frills and making them flake away.

TRIAL OF BURTON'S EMULSION PROCESS

W.K. Burton's paper, "On a Modified Gelatine Process", was read to the Photographic Society of Great Britain on 14 November 1882 at a meeting held in the Gallery of the Society of Painters in Water Colours at 5a Pall Mall East. As Captain Abney was absent, discussion of the process was deferred until the meeting on 12 December 1882. The paper was first published in the *Photographic Journal* on 5 December 1882 (New Series, Vol.11, pp.20-4). An editorial, "A Modified Method of Making Gelatine Paper", appeared in the *British Journal of Photography* on 17 November 1882 (p.651), and another, "Burton's New Method of Emulsification", on 24 November 1882 (p.667). The paper itself was reprinted in the *British Journal of Photography* on 15 December 1882 (pp.716-17).

The formula Burton recommended consisted of 340 grains of potassium bromide, 60 grains of gelatine, 2 minims of hydrochloric acid dissolved in 20 ounces of water, added to 400 grains of silver nitrate in crystals, 10 grains of potassium iodide dissolved in water, the whole boiled for between 40 and 90 minutes. After boiling, the emulsion was cooled to 120° Fahrenheit and ¾ ounce of ammonia and 1 ounce of alcohol were added to allow the precipitation of the bromide of silver to take place. This was left for about 48 hours, the liquid then being poured off and the beaker refilled with water. After the sensitive bromide had been stirred, it was left for a further 48 hours and the water was then poured off. 360 grains of gelatine, swelled in water and drained, were transferred to the beaker which was then left to stand for two or three days.

The advantages which Burton claimed for the process were plates of great sensitiveness and uniformity which were immune from green and red fog. The drawback was the length of time the process required. Another problem, which soon became apparent, was the appearance of a "superficial fog". The editor of the *British Journal of Photography* suggested that the amount of ammonia might be reduced, and Burton agreed. His "Superficial Fog on Gelatine Plates. Extension of the Period of Boiling", which appeared on 22 December (pp.730-1), acknowledged that prolonged boiling would achieve the same results and the ammonia might be reduced or even discarded.

Doyle's suggestion that alcohol might be added to neutralise the alkalinity of the emulsion and cure the "superficial fog" also met with Burton's approval. Two weeks later, he sent the *Journal* an article on "Precipitation Methods and Green Fog. Alcohol in Emulsion" (26 January 1883, p.45) which recommended the addition of alcohol and thanked Doyle for bringing the matter to his attention in his "Trial of Burton's Emulsion Process".

Although Doyle promised a further communication, it proved unnecessary as Burton followed up his suggestion and made the experiments himself.

SOUTHSEA: THREE DAYS IN SEARCH OF EFFECTS

The author admits that he is "The Doctor" so that it is his house,
Bush Villas, to which the group makes its way. The identity of the
other friends is less certain although various clues are given. "The
Man of Science" is described as "one of the leading dry-plate
workers of the day" and the profession of "The Lunatic" is given
as engineering. The former could well be W.K. Burton and, if this
were the case, "The Lunatic" could have been his brother, Cosmo
Innes Burton, who was both a photographer and engineer.
Alternatively it may have been the visit mentioned in Doyle's
letter when Burton had impressed Henry Greenwood with his
tales of what the two had done together in Edinburgh. In this case
"The Man of Science" could be Greenwood himself, though
Doyle would have had his tongue firmly in his cheek if the other
was W.K. Burton.

43   "Not angles, but angels,"] Venerable Bede, *Historia Eccles-
iastica*, II. i (said by Gregory I). It is traditionally quoted: "Non
Angli, sed Angeli".
44   not been honoured by a separate station] The Southsea
Improvement Association had called for a separate station in
October 1879. After protracted negotiations and the passage of
the necessary acts, the building was officially begun on 26 March
1884 and the line was opened on 1 July 1885. It ran from Fratton
to a terminus at Granada Road. It was never a success as the
connections were so slow that most passengers used the trams.
Traffic on the branch line ceased in 1914 and it was abandoned in
1923.
45   yachts were taken many times] Portsmouth and Ryde were
the principal centres for yachting in Britain, the home of the
Royal Portsmouth Corinthian Yacht Club, the Royal Albert Yacht
Club, and the Royal Victoria Yacht Club.
46   "The Doctor's" housekeeper . . . a charming little group of
Blenheim spaniels] The dogs may have been those which belonged to the housekeeper. Doyle placed an advertisement in
a local evening paper offering the basement in exchange for
services. From many applicants he chose Mrs. Smith who came

with a "sister" and some dogs. In *The Stark Munro Letters*, a semi-fictional account of these years, he describes the advent of the housekeeper as follows: "The first intimation I had was finding three little dogs in my hall. I had her up and explained that this was a breach of contract, and that I had no thoughts of running a menagerie. She pleaded very hard for her little dogs, which it seems are a mother and two daughters of some rare breed; so I at last gave in on the point."

The first housekeeper lasted a very short time: "She got intolerable so at last I told her I could not have it. She went away without a word of Goodbye, and what is more to the point without paying me one farthing and left me with all her bills on my hands." She was replaced by a kindly Scotchwoman who, according to the Rev. Elliot who taught Doyle's brother, "had been a servant to the family and was a mother both to him and to his little brother". If the dogs suggest the first, the character rather suggests the second housekeeper (who was, in all probability, the model for Sherlock Holmes' Mrs. Hudson).

48 the three forts erected by Lord Palmerston] Spitbank Fort, Horse Sand Fort, and No Man's Land Fort. These were built out at sea in shoal water as a result of the Royal Commission of 1859-60. At the same time a number of inland forts were constructed which became known as Palmerston's Follies.

49 Mr. Barnden, the well-known superintendant of the Gresham Life Insurance Society] George Barnden was the superintendent of the Gresham Life Assurance Society which had just established new offices in Southsea at Magdala House. He became a friend of Doyle's; both were members of the local Bowling Club. Doyle won the commission to perform medical examinations for the Society, and also seems to have written some verses called "The Lay of the Grasshopper" which served as an advertisement for it.

TO THE WATERFORD COAST AND ALONG IT

This account of a visit to Ireland during the summer of 1881 was written two years afterwards and was received by the *British Journal of Photography* at the end of July 1883.

Doyle went to Ireland in July 1881 to visit his relatives on his mother's side who lived at Lismore, a few miles from Youghal (pronounced "Yawl") on the Blackwater River. He was at the time preoccupied with various young ladies, Miss Jeffers and Miss Elmore Welden among them – the latter involving a close relationship which continued after he reached Southsea when she came to live at Ventnor on the Isle of Wight. The journey to Ireland provided the details for the article though the identity of the friends, if indeed they existed, is unclear. The use of the name Cunningham with the quotation from the Scottish poet, Allan Cunningham, suggests that they might have been created for the article.

Ireland was in a state of turbulence following a near famine in the West. The new Liberal Government under Gladstone had promised to ameliorate the suffering. William Edward Forster, the Chief Secretary of State for Ireland, introduced a Compensation for Disturbance Bill which was carried in the House of Commons during June 1880, but two months later it was rejected by a massive vote in the House of Lords. As a result the situation deteriorated. Parnell's Land League blamed Forster and there were a number of arrests and an abortive state trial in Dublin. So serious did the civil disorder become that the Government was forced to bring in a bill in January 1881 to give them the power to arrest people without trial. Forster was then the target for so many assassination attempts, his survival was, in some cases, remarkable. There were frequent reports of maiming and murder, while dynamite outrages became increasingly common both in Ireland and in Great Britain.

Doyle was a Liberal-Unionist, "a man whose general position was liberal, but who could not see his way to support Gladstone's Irish Policy" (*Memories and Adventures*, p.92). After his marriage, he played an active part in the Southsea Liberal Unionist Association and was for a time vice-president. In June 1886 he made a speech supporting the candidacy of Sir William Crossman who was standing as the Liberal Unionist for Portsmouth, and in June 1889 seconded the resolution thanking Balfour, the chief Secretary for Ireland, for his visit to Portsmouth. He stood for Parliament as a Liberal-Unionist in the Central Division of Edinburgh in 1900, though was defeated. In 1911, however, he came out in support of Home Rule believing that the situation had changed and that a strong, united, and independent Ireland within the Empire was preferable to a weak and divided Ireland within the Union.

51   my lodgings in the old metropolitan city of Scotland] Doyle

had lived with his parents in a shared house in George Square, Edinburgh, during his student days. But the address given in the *British Medical Directory* for 1882 is 15 Lonsdale Terrace, Edinburgh.

51 what Salisbury Cathedral was to Mr. Pecksniff] Dickens, *Martin Chuzzlewit*, II: "A young gentleman's premium being paid and the young gentleman come to Mr. Pecksniff's house . . . he improved himself for three or five years, according to his articles, in making elevations of Salisbury Cathedral from every possible sight." V: " 'You see, ' said Mr. Pecksniff, passing the candle rapidly from roll to roll of paper, 'some traces of our doings here. Salisbury Cathedral from the north. From the south. From the east. From the west. From the south-east. From the nor'-west.' "

52 Cook's tourist office] Thomas Cook had handled Doyle's visit to Europe in 1875 when he went to Feldkirch.

52 "down-trodden Clan-na-Gael"] The Clan-na-Gael was a society formed in 1873 by Fenians in America, whose object was to gain independence for Ireland. The headquarters were for a time in Chicago, but it had agents in England and Ireland who were responsible for assasinations and bomb outrages.

53 "He is a fellow of infinite chest"] *Hamlet*, IV.vii: "Alas! poor Yorick. I knew him, Horatio; a fellow of infinite jest, of most excellent fancy; . . ."

54 Arran . . . my friend Dr. Thompson] D.G. Thomson (*sic*), "The Island of Arran", *British Journal of Photography*, 30 September 1881, pp.504-5. David George Thomson was born in Edinburgh in 1856 and studied medicine at Edinburgh University where he graduated as an M.D. in 1881. He was for a time House surgeon at the Edinburgh Royal Infirmary which is where he would have met Doyle. Thomson used Doyle's photographs of skiing in Switzerland for an article on "Tobogganing and Ski-Running" in *Pearson's Magazine* (December 1897, Vol.4, pp.697-704) – there are nine illustrations by B. Schumacher "from Photographs by Dr. A. Conan Doyle".

54 a game of "Nap"] "Napoleon". A popular card game named after the Battle of Waterloo. A "Nap" or bid of five can be exceeded by a "Wellington" or a "Blucher" which are double and triple stakes.

55 "Won't you tell me why, Robin?"] A song with words and music by Claribel (pseud: Charlotte Alington Barnard), 1861.

56 the spot where some English conqueror had landed] Passage on the coast of Waterford Harbour was the landing place of Strongbow in 1170 when he came with a thousand men. Cromwell "came over" in August 1649 and landed at Dublin, going

north to Drogheda and then south to Wexford.

56   the first potato planted upon Irish soil] Sir Walter Raleigh, who had been granted 40,000 acres of land around Cork, Tipperary, and Youghal, brought the potato from America in 1586 and had it planted soon afterwards in his gardens at Youghal – a claim supported by a statement of Sir Robert Southwell to the Royal Society in 1693 that his grandfather had first cultivated the potato in Ireland from specimens given by Raleigh.

56   potatophagi] "potato-eaters" (Greek *-phagous*), as "anthropophagi".

57   topical song . . . "Buckshot Forster"] A song referring to W.E. Forster, Chief Secretary of State for Ireland (see above in the introductory note).

57   "a wet sheet and a flowing sea"] Allan Cunningham, *The Songs of Scotland, Ancient and Modern*, 1825, "A Wet Sheet and a Flowing Sea".

57   as Mark Twain said – the information which we did not possess would make a good size volume] *The Innocents Abroad*, VII: "The ancients considered the Pillars of Hercules the head of navigation and the end of the world. The information the ancients didn't have was very voluminous."

58   a round tower] The round tower at Ardmore is notable for the grotesque heads carved within where there is usually no decoration. The towers are now believed to have been built as belfries which could also serve as places of refuge. The ruins nearby are of the monastic settlement of St. Declan founded in the seventh century, the Oratory being an interesting example of an early church.

At a meeting of the Portsmouth Literary and Scientific Society on 14 February 1888 at which R.W. Ball, the architect who was later to design Doyle's house at Hindhead, spoke about "English Homes", Doyle asked the lecturer "to what he ascribed the origin of the Irish round towers. They were older, he believed, than the wattled huts of the Saxons, or the works of the Romans, and their origin was shrouded in uncertainty. They were built of a peculiarly hard stone, which was cemented together in such a way as to give the impression that the constructors were a people who had some knowledge of building" (*Hampshire County Times*, 15 February 1888). Mr. Ball in replying attributed the origin of the Irish Towers to Norman builders.

59   "the sort of thing no fellah would understand"] Possibly a reference to the young fellow called John in *The Professor at the Breakfast Table* whose favourite turn of phrase it resembles: "Sometimes a fellah feels lonely, and would like to have a nice

young woman, to tell her how lonely he feels"; "Fetch on the
fellah that makes them long words! – he said, – and planted a
straight hit with the right fist in the concave palm of the left hand
. . ."

59 a meteoric stone] St. Declan's stone is a glacial boulder
believed to cure rheumatism.

59 Queenstown] On the Great Island at the mouth of the Lee
below Cork. It was an important British naval base with the fleet
anchorage in the land-locked harbour known as the Cove of
Cork, and was the port from which many emigrant ships sailed
for America. It has since been renamed Cobh (pronounced
"Cove").

A DAY ON "THE ISLAND"

The trip took place during the early spring of 1884. Doyle visited
the Isle of Wight at this time with his sisters, Annette and Lottie,
and his friend, Jessie Drummond. He mentions it in a letter to
Jessie's mother: "One day we had the Government steamer and
went over all the forts in the Solent. Then we prolonged our
voyage to Seaview in the Isle of Wight and had a charming lunch
in a little hotel and came back at our leisure – a very enjoyable
day."

Johnson, whose identity is unclear though he may have been
based on Doyle's school friend, James Ryan, left Waterloo (or, at
least, is described as having done so) on the 7.05 train which
reached Portsmouth Town at 9.32 and then made its way to
Portsmouth Harbour where the schooner *Victoria* waited. The
ship, launched in 1881 and the first on the route built of steel,
passed along the shore to Southsea Pier and then across the
Solent to Ryde. With the growth of tourism the route had become
seriously overcrowded and two new vessels began operating in
April 1884.

Ryde was one of the first places in England to have a pier, a
right acquired by an Act of Parliament in 1812. Forty years later,
the competition from the short-lived Isle of Wight Ferry Company goaded the Ryde Pier Company into improving the struc-
ture and providing a new pier along the eastern side which
carried a single-track tramway. In 1864, 1876, and from 1881-
1884 the trams were operated by steam. During the last period so
much damage was done to the pier that it was necessary to replace

the two steam locomotive cars with horse-drawn trams, which were used until March 1886 when electric trams were introduced.

Doyle may have been influenced in the choice of his title by a description in *The Autocrat at the Breakfast Table* of "the Island", II: "Where have I been for the last three or four days? Down at the Island, . . . The Island is where? No matter. It is the most splendid domain that any man looks upon in these latitudes."

60 "fresh fields and pastures new"] Milton, *Lycidas*, l.193: "Tomorrow to fresh woods, and pastures new."
61 the "Victory" (the old flagship of Nelson), the "Duke of Wellington," and the "St. Vincent."] The *Victory*, which was launched at Chatham in May 1765, was Nelson's flagship at St. Vincent (1797) and Trafalgar (1805). It was moored opposite the Portsmouth Harbour Terminus and was open to the public. The *St. Vincent* lay to its south and was used as a training ship. The *Duke of Wellington* (later replaced by the *Inflexible*) lay to the north and served as the port guard-ship.
62 Blue Posts Hotel] This was named after the original inn, built in 1613, which had large wooden pilasters painted bright blue flanking the entrances to the bar and the stable yard. It had been made famous by Captain Marryat whose Midshipman Easy and Peter Simple frequented it.
62 the towers of Osborne] Osborne House was built in 1846 and became the favourite residence of Queen Victoria, who spent about thirteen weeks of the year here over Christmas and during August for Cowes Week.
63 the venerable castle of Carisbrooke in which Charles I was imprisoned] Charles I crossed the Solent on 11 November 1647; he was made a prisoner the following month and held at Carisbrooke until 1 December 1648.
63 the Roman antiquities . . . at Brading] The Roman villa was discovered when an amateur archaeologist heard two children arguing over potsherds, and it was excavated in 1880. It has twelve rooms, some with plain tessellated floors and others with mosaics including one of Orpheus and another showing the Seasons.

The villa was probably mentioned at the Portsmouth Literary and Scientific Society meeting on 15 January 1884 which Doyle attended. C. Foran gave a lecture entitled "Archaeological Notes and Antiquarian Notes of Hampshire".
64 numerous monoliths – long perpendicular stones erected upon the summits of hills] These are twelve burial mounds of the Bronze Age at Ashey Down, a mile or two from Brading.

64   *"sub tegmine fagi"*] Virgil, *Eclogues*, I, l.1: "Tityre, tu patulae recubans sub tegmine fagi/silvestrem tenui musam meditaris avena . . ." (Tityrus, . . . you lie there at ease under the awning of a spreading beech and practise country songs on a light shepherd's pipe . . .' – E.V. Rieu).

64   densely unconscious that he is about to be endowed with a franchise] The Third Reform Bill of 1884 was to extend the borough household suffrage of 1867 to the counties. It had been promised by the Liberals under Gladstone in the election manifesto of 1880.

64   Shanklin Chine] A fissure in the cliffs about 60 yards wide and 100 yards deep, made by a falling stream.

EASTER MONDAY WITH A CAMERA

The Volunteer Review, described in this article, was held on 14 April 1884. It was the first volunteer display at Portsmouth which Doyle saw, though a similar event had been held two years before.

To mark the occasion triumphal arches were erected in Portsmouth and in the surrounding villages. There was one at the High Street end of the Cambridge Road and another in Commercial Road. There were also hundreds of flags on loan from the Dockyard and bunting on many of the public buildings. The arch in Commercial Road was judged to be the most effective; it was illuminated at night by electricity and bore a representation of the British coat of arms with the mottoes "One Volunteer is Worth Two Pressed Men" and "A Hearty Welcome to England's Manhood". Similar mottoes were to be found elsewhere; there was one, for example, on an evergreen arch at the entrance to the United Services Recreation Ground which complimented the Prince and Princess of Saxe-Weimar.

Over twenty thousand soldiers took part, of whom the majority were volunteers. The general idea was of two forces, a Western Force moving from Salisbury to reinforce the garrison at Hilsea and a Northern Force coming from Guildford to intercept the movement. The Western Force, represented by the Volunteer Corps, was detrained at Fareham where it was joined by an Infantry Brigade from Gosport, and a Field Battery; the Northern Force of volunteers was detrained at Havant; and the Hilsea Garrison was formed by regular troops.

Although Portsmouth was usually the scene of naval reviews,

on this occasion the sea was considered not to exist. A pontoon bridge had been thrown across the canal between the Hilsea Lines and the neighbourhood of Cosham to enable the garrison to make a sortie. From eight o'clock in the morning the residents of Portsmouth and Southsea made their way to Portsdown Hill, then at twelve o'clock when the umpires were in position, a signal gun was fired and the battle began. There were a number of separate skirmishes, some hindered by the crowds of onlookers and carriages. One civilian was knocked down by an uncontrolled horse, opposing groups of cavalry passed within yards of each other without realising because of the spectators, and one group opened fire on its own lines. But the occasion passed off successfully and after an hour and fifty minutes the cease-fire sounded. The troops then prepared for the march past which took place half a mile west of Fort Widley at a position marked by the Royal Standard. The spectators had begun moving towards the spot before the cease-fire; when it sounded there was a rush which completely swept away the enclosure set apart for the civilian dignitaries. At three o'clock the Duke of Cambridge took up his position in the saluting box with other military personnel. The Commander-in-Chief, Prince Edward of Saxe-Weimar, passed and then joined the Duke, while the regiments and their bands marched by.

The two Nordenfeldt guns aroused particular interest. Designed by a Swedish engineer, though built in England, the gun had been demonstrated at Portsmouth two years before. It was eventually chosen as a replacement for the recently introduced Gardner gun, and was only superseded by the famous Maxim gun. On this occasion the Nordenfeldts were mounted on the patent gun carriages designed by Colonel Alt.

Doyle went with his sisters, Annette and Lottie, and his friend Jessie Drummond to watch a review during 1884, but it is described in a letter to his mother as occurring on a Saturday and was probably a naval review. On this occasion he may have been accompanied by his younger brother, Innes, who had been fascinated by the soldiers and sailors ever since his arrival at Southsea. Doyle had quickly learnt to live with his brother's miniature reviews. "I never come near him," he told his mother, "that I don't get one over the head with a cutlass in his character of 'The leader of the boarding party' or else a prod from a bayonet in his never-sufficiently-to-be-execrated part of the 'first man in the trenches'." Innes later joined the army and by the time of his death in 1919 held the rank of Brigadier-General.

The sight of the massive volunteer army may have had an

influence on Doyle's later thought. At the time of the Boer War he applied to the War Office and to the Middlesex Yeomanry seeking a commission, and when this was refused accepted the offer of a post as a volunteer doctor in Langman's field hospital. After his return from South Africa, he campaigned on behalf of civilian riflemen and for the establishment of rifle clubs throughout the country. It was a subject to which he turned with renewed vigour in 1914 when he set up a Civilian National Reserve at Crowborough. He decided to do so on 4 August 1914, and two days later had one hundred and forty men under drill who were ready to start rifle practice on the following day. The Reserve was disbanded shortly afterwards, but was revived in a slightly different form. Doyle was enrolled on 21 July 1916 as Private V184343 of the 5th Volunteer Battalion of the Royal Sussex Regiment and was discharged on 25 September 1919.

66   like Hal of the Wynd] A battle to settle a quarrel between two clans was fought before the king on the North Inch of Perth in 1392. Each was to have thirty men, but one man was lacking, so a local smith, Henry Wynd, agreed to act as a substitute. He fought well without knowing which side he was acting for. "To fight for your own hand, like Henry Wynd" soon became a proverb. The episode is referred to in Scott's *Rob Roy*, and forms a conspicuous part of his subsequent novel *The Fair Maid of Perth*.
68   Paley's *Evidences of Christianity*] William Paley's *View of the Evidences of Christianity* (1794) is a compendium of orthodox arguments in refutation of the deists.
71   4th Dragoon Guards – the heroes of the Kassassin charge] The charge took place in September 1882, shortly before the taking of Tel-el-Kebir. Doyle followed the Egyptian campaigns with interest and pasted a number of press reports into his first scrapbook. He was later a special correspondent for the *Westminster Gazette* in Egypt during the early part of 1896.

ARRAN IN AUTUMN

Doyle's earliest visit to Arran was in 1877 when he was surprised to meet Dr. Joseph Bell whose special "weakness" was grouse shooting in September. The island had been popular with tourists for some time. Robert Browning had been there in 1862 after the death of his wife Elizabeth, and it was the favourite retreat of Sir

Noel Paton whose presence had brought Lewis Carroll, a great photographer of the collodion period. Carroll wanted Paton to do the illustrations for *Through the Looking-Glass*. Doyle never met Lewis Carroll, though his uncle had done so at the beginning of 1867 when the idea of illustrating the Alice book had been discussed.

The visit described in the article would have taken place in the autumn of 1884. In September, to choose a month at random, the trains from Glasgow (St. Enoch) to Ardrossan left at 8.40 am and 4.30 pm daily. They connected with the saloon steamer *Brodick Castle*, owned by William Buchanan, which called first at Brodick and then at Lamlash. There was also a service to Whiting Bay. The pier, on which a toll was levied, at Brodick had been built in 1873, that at Lamlash in 1883.

Brodick Castle was the seat of the Dukes of Hamilton. It had been extended by the addition of a new wing in 1844 and the village of Brodick had been moved away from the vicinity of the castle in 1856. Red deer were introduced when deer-stalking and grouse shooting became popular as a result of the Queen's example at Balmoral. In 1884 the title had passed to the twelfth Duke of Hamilton who was the last of the direct line.

Doyle uses Arran as the background for two of his uncollected stories, "Touch and Go: A Midshipman's Story" and "Our Midnight Visitor".

73   guide-books and *Bradshaws*] The tourist literature about the island of Arran was somewhat limited. There were a few general guidebooks like Black's *Picturesque Tourist of Scotland* which was published in Edinburgh, Walter Scott's poem "The Lord of the Isles", a Wordsworthian poem by David Landsborough entitled "Arran, a Poem in Six Cantos" and a prose work by the same author, *Excursion in Arran*. The *Bradshaw*, a complete timetable of train services and connecting ferries, was first published in 1839 and quickly became a *sine qua non* for Victorian travellers. Although Sherlock Holmes describes the vocabulary of *Bradshaw* as "nervous and terse, but limited" (*The Valley of Fear*), Doyle made full use of the information it contained and many of the details in these articles are derived from it.

74   Horatio McCullough] 1805-67. An artist who dominated Scottish landscape painting at this period. His painting of the Highlands were in great demand.

74   Waller Paton] 1828-95. An industrious worker and copious exhibitor. His prettily detailed landscapes enjoyed enormous popularity with the general, as distinguished from the art, public.

Doyle may well have been at the opening of the Royal Scottish Academy in the spring of 1879 where he would have seen the work of the artists he mentioned, as he refers to it in "John Barrington Cowles", a short story which was published in 1884.

74 "Every prospect pleases and only man is vile"] Bishop Heber's hymn, "From Greenland's Icy Mountains".

74 Fullarton] The Fullarton link with the island began shortly before 1371 with the grant of Tonnridire by Robert, the High Steward, and thereafter the family held many important administrative positions. Doyle may have been given an introduction to Mrs. Fullarton by Dr. Thomson who was both a friend and a photographer. Thomson had described Arran in 1881 in a similar article for the *British Journal of Photography* (see notes for "To the Waterford Coast and Along It"). There may also be a connection between Mrs. Fullarton and Miss Jessie Fullarton, who was elected as a member of the Edinburgh Photographic Society on 7 May 1879.

A NEW SCIENTIFIC SUBJECT

The correspondence on the psychic force "Od" forms a small part of the contemporary debate on colour and the possibility of its reproduction. W. Harding Warner offered many diverse ideas in his frequent letters to the photographic journals, of which most were based on an imperfect grasp of science and a superficially wide reading. The "Odic Force" to which he refers was suggested by the experiments made in Germany by Baron Carl von Reichenbach (1788-1869) who published his findings as *Odisch-Magnetische Briefe* (Letters on Od and Magnetism) in 1852 and 1856, *Der Sensitive Mensch und Sein Verhalten zum Ode* (The Sensitive Man and His Relation to Od) in 1854 and 1855, and other shorter studies.

Doyle's reply would have been a cause of embarrassment later in his life, for the arguments and the flippancy of tone are similar to those used by critics of psychic photography, of which he was to become an advocate. His own interest in psychic phenomena began a few years later (his first letter on spiritualism was published in 1887), but it was not until 1916 that he dedicated his life to the subject. He was then often at loggerheads with scientists and would use Baron Reichenbach in his own defence, quoting the aphorism that "there is a scientific incredulity which exceeds in stupidity the obtuseness of a clodhopper". His criticism of Warner's "men of science" was also used against him on a number of occasions. Joseph McCabe, for example, after the Queen's Hall debate on "The Truth of Spiritualism" in 1920 urged him to give the names of the ten university professors whom he claimed had accepted the validity of spiritualism.

The reference to the heat generated by the taxgatherer is perhaps an allusion to Doyle's experience with his first income tax form which was sent back to him with the words "Most unsatisfactory". He returned it having added underneath "I entirely agree", and the result was a personal visit from the tax man. Although the problem was resolved, his dislike was not lessened. A contemporary letter is cut short in the following way. "I see a taxgatherer coming down the road, so must conclude before crawling under the table"; and as late as 1889, he wrote to the Portsmouth *Evening News* to complain about the injustice of the system under which a taxpayer's return could be ignored.

81 Wm. Brooks, in a recent number of the Journal, . . . *Effects of Contact or Pressure on the Sensitive Salts of Silver*] British Journal of Photography, 22 June 1883, pp.357-8.

83 the very early numbers of *Chamber's Edinburgh Journal*] "Actino-Chemistry", *Chambers's Edinburgh Journal*, 28 December 1844, pp.403-6. Other papers on the early photographic processes appeared on 30 March 1839 and 3 December 1842.

84 Artemus Ward's description of the silver mine] Mark Twain, "First Interview with Artemus Ward". Twain's account of a visit to Ward, who first offered him a strong whisky cocktail and then proceeded to describe the Nebraska silver mines which left Twain more and more confused until he realised that he was the victim of a joke "in the way of a string of plausibly worded sentences that didn't mean anything under the sun".

85 the all-comprehensive syllable of the Hindoos, "Om"] Oliver Wendell Holmes, *The Professor at the Breakfast-Table*, I: "Take that famous word, O'm, of the Hindoo mythology. Even a priest cannot pronounce it without sin; and a holy Pundit would shut his ears and run away from you in horror, if you should say it aloud. What do you care for O'm?" Holmes is discussing the religious currency of mankind which, he says, consists entirely of polarised words. "Borrow one . . . and you will find it leaves all its magnetism behind it."

86 a certain well-known temperance organisation] There were six main temperance organisations whose members wore various

coloured uniforms and ribbons – probably the best-known being the "blue ribbon". They were the British Temperance League, The Band of Hope, the United Kingdom Alliance, the National Temperance League, the Church of England Total Abstinence Society, and the Independent Order of Good Templars. Although Doyle would have seen the organisations marching through the streets of Portsmouth, which had a major problem with drink, he was also well versed in the subject. One of his earliest articles was entitled "On the Intemperance of Our Country", and he had witnessed the disastrous effects of drink on his own father.

SOURCES

British Journal of Photography

A. CONAN DOYLE

"After Cormorants with a Camera", xxviii, 14, 21 October 1881, 533-4, 544-6.

"On the Slave Coast with a Camera", xxix, 31 March, 7 April 1882, 185-7, 202-3.

"Up an African River with the Camera", xxix, 28 July 1882, 431-2.

"Dry Plates on a Wet Moor", xxix, 3 November 1882, 627-9.

"A Few Technical Hints", *British Journal Photographic Almanac*, 1883, 91-2.

"Trial of Burton's Emulsion Process", xxx, 12 January 1883, 20.

"Southsea: Three Days in Search of Effects", xxx, 22 June 1883, 359-61.

"The 'New' Scientific Subject", xxx, 20 July 1883, 418.

"To the Waterford Coast and Along It", xxx, 17, 24 August 1883, 481-2, 497-8.

"A Day on 'The Island' ", xxxi, 25 April 1884, 268-9.

"Easter Monday with the Camera", xxxi, 23 May 1884, 330-2

"Arran in Autumn", xxxii, 17 July 1885, 459-60.

"With a Camera on an African River", xxxii, 30 October 1885, 697.

W. HARDING WARNER "A New Scientific Subject", xxx, 13 July
1883, 405-6.
"A New Scientific Subject", xxx, 27 July
1883, 440.
A. BROTHERS "A New Scientific Subject", xxx, 20 July
1883, 425.
"The Voyage to West Africa" is taken from A. Conan Doyle's
autobiography, *Memories and Adventures* (London, 1924, pp.47-
57).

BIBLIOGRAPHY

A. CONAN DOYLE: *The Firm of Girdlestone*, London, 1890; *The
Adventures of Sherlock Holmes*, London, 1892; *The Stark Munro
Letters*, London, 1895; *The Wanderings of a Spiritualist*, London,
1921; *The Case for Spirit Photography*, London, 1922; *The Coming of
the Fairies*, London, 1922 (rev. ed., 1928); *Our Second American
Adventure*, London, 1924; *Memories and Adventures*, London, 1924
(rev. ed., 1930); *The History of Spiritualism*, 2 vols., London, 1926.
"The Recollections of Captain Wilkie"–*Chambers's Journal*, 19, 26
January 1895; "The Combermere Photograph" – *Quarterly
Transactions of the British College of Psychic Science*, October 1926.

Miscellaneous and Biographical: "A Day with Dr. Conan Doyle"
by Harry How, *Strand Magazine*, August 1892; "Tobogganing
and Ski-Running" by D.G. Thomson, With Illustrations from
Photographs by Dr. A. Conan Doyle, *Pearson's Magazine*, Decem-
ber 1897; "The Unionist Candidate for Central Edinburgh",
Evening Dispatch, Edinburgh 28 September 1900 [on his friend-
ship with Mary Burton]; "Novelist, Spiritualist and Humanit-
arian, Conan Doyle – The Creator of Sherlock Holmes. A Visit to
His Home at Bignell Wood" by John Lewis, *Cape Argus*, 27
October 1928; Obituary note, *British Journal of Photography*, 11
July 1930. *Conan Doyle: His Life and Art* by Hesketh Pearson,
London, 1943; *The Life of Sir Arthur Conan Doyle*, by John Dickson
Carr, London, 1949; *Conan Doyle*, by Pierre Nordon, 1966 (from
the French).

W.K. BURTON: [Cosmo Innes and . . .] *Sanitary Inspection of Dwelling Houses*, London, 1880; *The ABC of Modern Photography*, London, 1882 (*Burton's Modern Photography* from 1885); *Practical Guide to Photographic and Photo-Mechanical Printing*, London, 1887; *Optics for Photographers*, London, 1891; [John Milne and . . .] *The Great Earthquake in Japan, 1891*, (2nd ed.) Yokohama & London, 1894; *The Water Supply of Towns and the Construction of Waterworks*, London 1894.

Miscellaneous and Biographical: *The Book Hunter* by John Hill Burton (with a Memoir of the Author by Katherine Burton), New Edition, Edinburgh, 1882 [on his youth]; *Out of Doors Life in Japan*. Photographed by W.K. Burton, Yokohama, 1893; Obituary, *British Journal of Photography*, 22 September 1899; Memoir, *Proceedings of the Institute of Civil Engineers*, cxxxix, 373.